T0035065
R.I.P.

R.I.P.

Cursed Objects

Cursed Objects

Strange but True Stories of the World's Most Infamous Items

J. W. Ocker

QUIRK BOOKS
PHILADELPHIA

Library of Congress Cataloging-in-Publication Data
Names: Ocker, J. W., author.
Title: Cursed objects : strange but true stories of the world's most infamous items / J. W. Ocker.
Description: Philadelphia : Quirk Books, 2020. | Includes bibliographical references and index. | Summary: "Illustrated compendium telling the stories of real-life cursed objects from throughout history"—Provided by publisher.
Identifiers: LCCN 2020011595 (print) | LCCN 2020011596 (ebook) | ISBN 9781683692362 (trade paperback) | ISBN 9781683692379 (epub)
Subjects: LCSH: Cursed objects.
Classification: LCC BF1442.C87 O25 2020 (print) | LCC BF1442.C87 (ebook) | DDC 001.94—dc23
LC record available at https://lccn.loc.gov/2020011595
LC ebook record available at https://lccn.loc.gov/2020011596

ISBN: 978-1-68369-236-2

Printed in China

Typeset in Goudy Old Style, Goudy Sans, and Tremolo
Designed by Ryan Hayes
Illustrations by Jon MacNair
Production management by John J. McGurk

Quirk Books
215 Church Street
Philadelphia, PA 19106
quirkbooks.com

10 9 8 7 6 5 4 3

Dedicated to
Rebecca Gyllenhaal,
for sending me on
this adventure

Contents

VI. Why Aren't These Objects Cursed?

VII. The Curse in the Machine

R.I.P.
R.I.P.
R.I.P.
R.I.P.
R.I.P.
R.I.P.

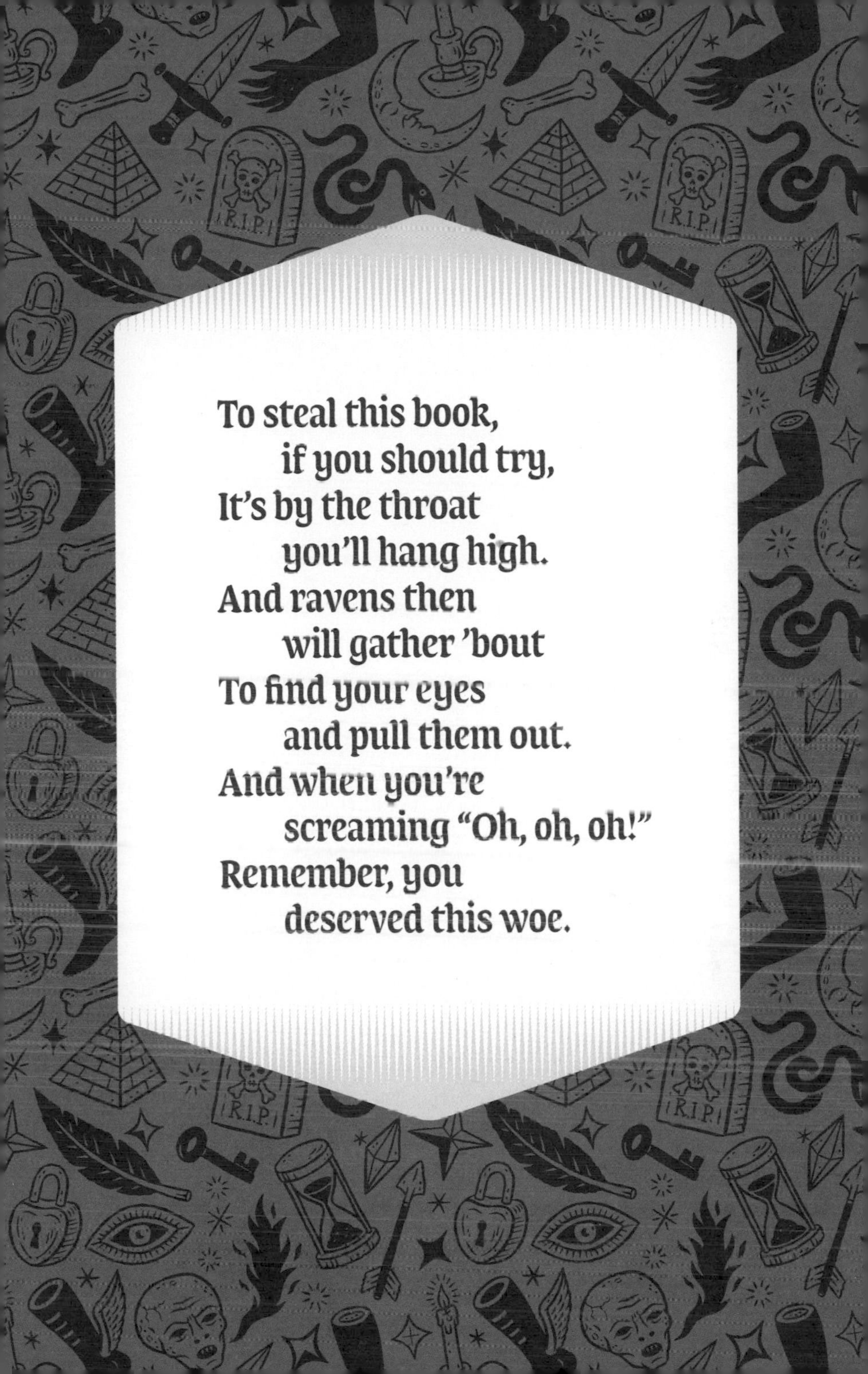
To steal this book,
if you should try,
It's by the throat
you'll hang high.
And ravens then
will gather 'bout
To find your eyes
and pull them out.
And when you're
screaming "Oh, oh, oh!"
Remember, you
deserved this woe.
R.I.P.
R.I.P.
R.I.P.
R.I.P.

Headfirst into the Accursed

I hate to be the one to tell you this, but many seemingly innocuous objects will make your life suck. They might even kill you. We call these objects cursed. A cursed object could be a vase, a chair, a painting, a doll: things we all have around our houses, in our attics and basements. They could be in museums, separated from the general populace by a thin piece of glass. They could be out in the open — masquerading as ordinary statues or rocks, for instance. Anything can be cursed, and you rarely know until it's too late. Good thing you have this book to help you.

So what is a cursed object? In lore, it's an inanimate item that brings misfortune, harm, or death to its owners or those with whom it comes in contact. An object can become cursed because someone with powerful and mystical knowledge hexes it. Or it could have been present at a scene of great tragedy, absorbing dark energy like a battery and powering other tragedies going forward. It could be inherently evil from the start, all the way down to its MADE IN CHINA sticker. Or it could all just be in our heads.

You don't have to believe in cursed objects to be fascinated by them. Because another, less paranormal definition of a cursed object is an object that gathers stories to itself – and more specifically, tragedies. Objects are intimately connected to people. We make them, live with them, use them, love them, and are sometimes even buried with them, and people continuously find themselves in the midst of tragedy. Cursed objects are those items that have simply been the mute witnesses to more tragedies than other items. They then become devices for remembering those stories and provide opportunities for retelling them.

And don't get me wrong. There's magic in that, too: that a simple oak chair, out of millions of oak chairs in the world, would be connected to so many stories of misfortune and death (see Busby's Stoop Chair, page 123). The idea that cursed objects operate as storytelling mechanisms for tragedy in culture is at the heart of this book, although that doesn't mean we won't have fun with the notion that there might be other, less explainable, and more sinister forces at work.

In this book, we'll look at crystal skulls and creepy dolls, tiny stone heads and ancient weapons. We'll cover the infamous, including Annabelle the Doll (page 173) and the Hope Diamond (page 18), as well as the obscure. Ever heard of the Little Mannie with His Daddy's Horns (page 134)? Probably not. I've risked visiting a few firsthand for you. I even brought one into my home. We'll dip into the business of cursed objects, where *cursed* is prized as a marketing term and cursed objects are collected, displayed in museums, and even sold on eBay. We'll learn that even technology and digital artifacts can be cursed.

Before we begin, we'll need to define some terms. *Cursed* is often used synonymously with *haunted* and *possessed*, but these three qualities are distinct. For our purposes, the difference is one of intelligence. Cursed items have none. They're objects that have become bad luck via someone who has purposefully cursed them or by happenstance. By contrast, a haunted object has a spirit intelligence attached directly to it, and a possessed item is similarly inhabited, in this case by a demonic entity (although some say that an object cannot technically be possessed, only humans can . . . lucky us). Both haunted and possessed objects can function practically as cursed objects if they bring misfortune to enough people, but if they merely act spooky, then they're not cursed.

Take, for instance, the wedding dress of Anna Baker at the Baker Mansion History Museum in Altoona, Pennsylvania, or the haunted mirror at the Myrtles Plantation in St. Francisville, Louisiana. Both objects are mentioned regularly in articles about cursed items. But stories of the Anna Baker wedding dress mostly involve the dress moving around on its own and the specter of its owner popping up here and there. The haunted mirror at the Myrtles Plantation reflects creepy figures and sometimes appears smudged with ghostly handprints. Both objects are spooky as hell, but neither causes the serial misfortune that a cursed object is supposed to.

For the purposes of this book, I've also ruled out cursed objects without detailed curse stories. For instance, the Villa Zorayda Museum in St. Augustine, Florida, displays an Egyptian rug made entirely out of cat hair that was once wrapped around a mummified human foot (also on display). Some posit that it's the oldest existing rug. Others posit that it's cursed and that anyone who steps on the rug will die (hence why the rug is currently hung on a wall). However, its entire curse story was contained in those three sentences. A fascinating object, but difficult to wring a narrative essay out of.

Now, more than objects can be cursed. People can. Places can. But for the purposes of this journey, I'm interested in objects that are cursed. I generally followed the terrifying maxim, "Could I inadvertently pick it up at a flea market or an antiques store and bring it into my home?" or, "Could I brush up against it in a museum and be forever damned?" And, with a handful of notable exceptions, that's exactly what is included in this book.

So, beware. Because it's not just ancient artifacts looted from old coffins buried deep in exotic climes that will ruin your life. It could also be the "I Hate Mondays" coffee mug on your desk that your mom bought you at a garage sale.

Cursed under Glass

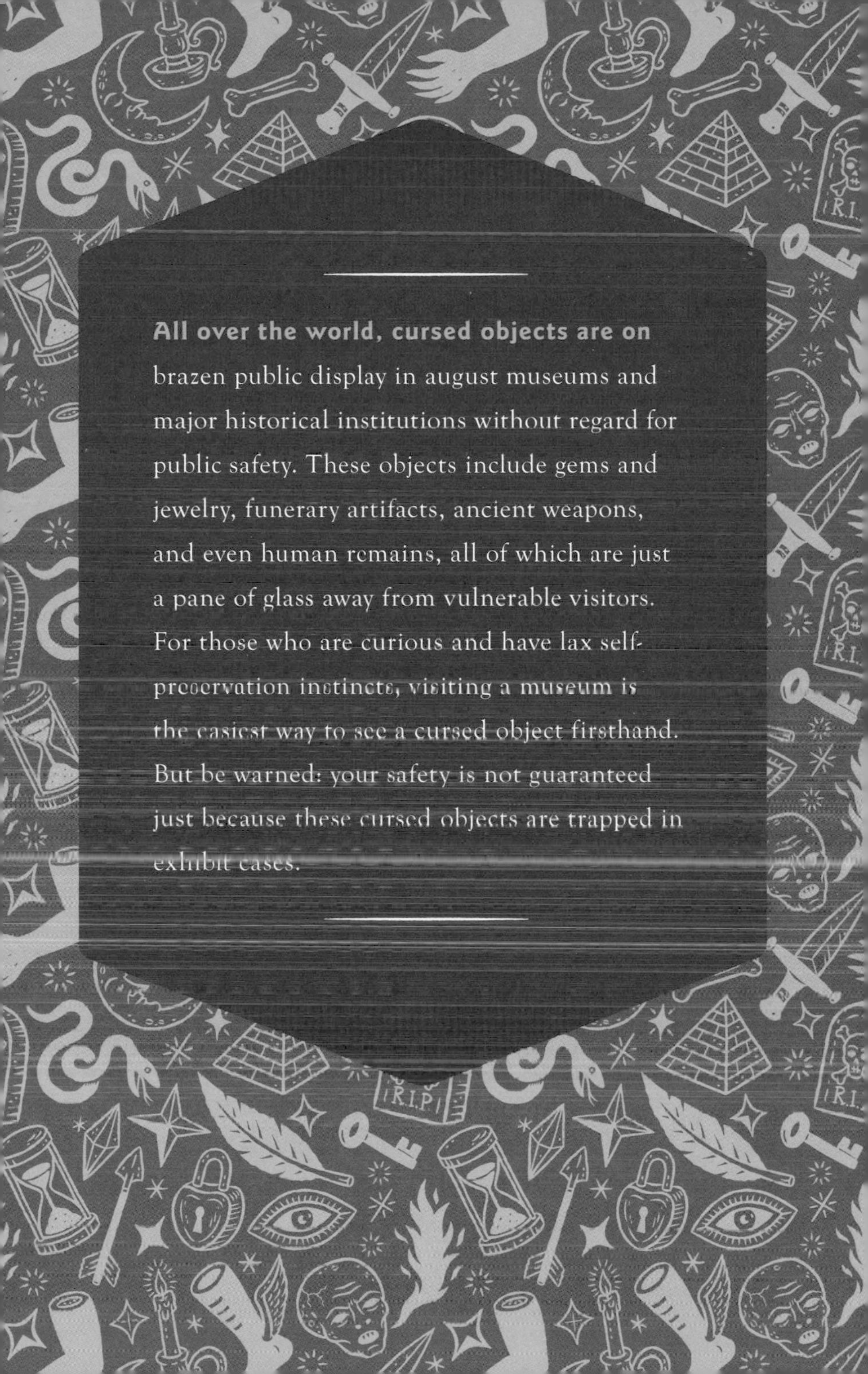

All over the world, cursed objects are on brazen public display in august museums and major historical institutions without regard for public safety. These objects include gems and jewelry, funerary artifacts, ancient weapons, and even human remains, all of which are just a pane of glass away from vulnerable visitors. For those who are curious and have lax self-preservation instincts, visiting a museum is the easiest way to see a cursed object firsthand. But be warned: your safety is not guaranteed just because these cursed objects are trapped in exhibit cases.

The Hope Diamond

PLACE OF ORIGIN: KOLLUR MINE, INDIA	**ESTIMATED VALUE:** \$200 MILLION–\$350 MILLION
NOTABLE OWNERS: KING LOUIS XIV, KING LOUIS XVI, HENRY PHILIP HOPE, PIERRE CARTIER, EVALYN WALSH MCLEAN	**CURRENT LOCATION:** SMITHSONIAN NATIONAL MUSEUM OF NATURAL HISTORY, WASHINGTON, DC

It was ripped from the eye of a cyclopean Hindu idol in India. It ended the French monarchy. It was the ruin of members of the new American aristocracy. The people who have owned or worn it have been ripped apart by dogs, shot, beheaded, pushed over cliffs, starved to death, and drowned aboard sinking ships. It has caused suicides, madness, and the death of children. It killed Rod Serling. It inspired the fictional Heart of the Ocean gem in James Cameron's film *Titanic*.

It is the Hope Diamond, and it is cursed.

Weighing 45.52 carats, the Hope Diamond is the world's largest blue diamond. It is the platonic ideal of a cursed object. It has an exotic origin and a history that spans centuries, yet it is small enough to fit in a pocket. To steal. To lose. To disappear. It is valuable enough to be bought and traded and stolen in the rarified atmosphere of throne rooms and private jets. Many have owned it, and the chain of provenance sometimes reads like an expensive game of hot potato.

And, of course, tragedies have paralleled and entwined its entire timeline.

However, all of the commonly circulated claims mentioned in the first paragraph of this chapter – except for the *Titanic* bit – are unverifiable. But that doesn't matter. The real story of the Hope Diamond, including how it came to be considered cursed, is just as fascinating.

Its story starts a billion years ago some one hundred miles below the Earth's crust. Primal forces crushed carbon into a hunk of crystal. It was a common process at the time. But something rare happened in this case. The element boron fused into the crystal's structure, turning the gem a deep

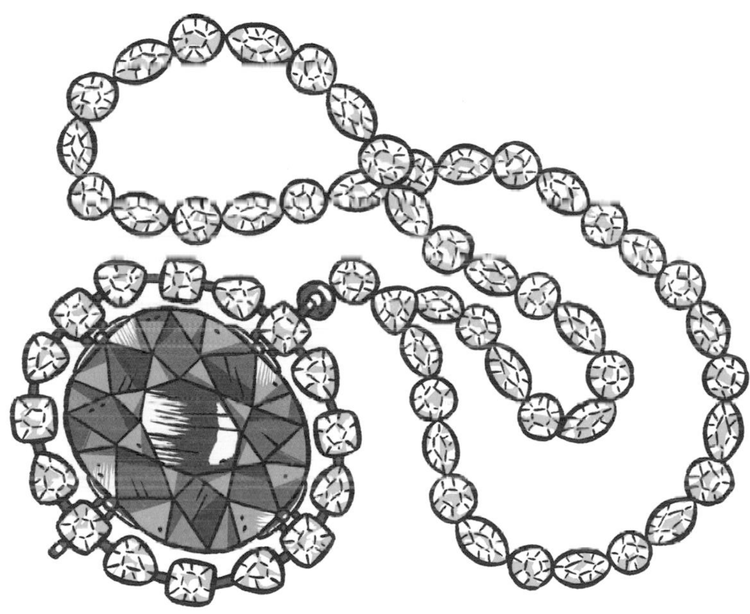

ocean blue. Eventually volcanic activity forced the rock close to the surface of what would one day be called India, where it was pulled from the ground hundreds of years ago by India's legendary mining industry.

India was once thought to be the only source of diamonds on the planet. And that's why a pioneering French merchant named Jean-Baptiste Tavernier made six epic journeys there in the mid-seventeenth century. On one of those journeys, he came into possession of a heart-shaped, 112-carat, rough-cut blue diamond that came out of the Kollur Mine. The stone would eventually be called the Tavernier Violet (*violet* was a synonym for *blue* at the time). Contrary to the legend, he attained it not by stealing it from the eye of a god (although he saw plenty of jewel-eyed gods in the temples of India), but through the usual channels of trade.

Tavernier sold the stone to King Louis XIV of France, along with more than one thousand other diamonds. But that large blue gem was obviously special. It accounted for about 25 percent of the price of the entire lot. Tavernier would go on not to be ripped apart by dogs, as some say, but to relax from his life of adventure near the shores of Lake Geneva. He would later come out of retirement, but still lived comfortably into his eighties.

Louis XIV also lived a long life. Under his watch, the future Hope Diamond was cut down and refined into a more glittery and fashionable 67 carats. By then it was called the French Blue and was considered an important part of the French crown jewels.

Those jewels were passed down without much drama until the reign of King Louis XVI, who held the throne during the French Revolution, an uprising that eventually left him and his wife, Marie Antoinette, without their heads. The Hope Diamond is blamed by some for Marie Antionette's death, although she almost certainly never wore it. She loved diamonds, but the French Blue was reserved for her husband. It was set in an insignia for one of his orders and only removed once from its setting during that time, for scientific examination. The French monarchy dissolved after the revolution, and in 1792, the French Blue was stolen and lost to history . . . temporarily.

Some scholars believe that the French Blue was used to bribe Charles Ferdinand, the Duke of Brunswick, Germany, not to invade France. Much of Europe was terrified that the revolution in France would spread to their countries and had armies at the ready to help stifle potential conflict. However it happened, the diamond surfaced again two decades later, this time in England, in the possession of a gem merchant named Daniel Eliason. It had been cut down again, this time to 44 carats (about the size of a walnut), possibly in an effort to disguise it from Napoleon, who would have wanted to reunite it with the French crown jewels.

From there it possibly came into the possession of King George IV of the United Kingdom for a time, but by 1839, it belonged to a wealthy London banking family named Hope. And that's how it got a name that seems straight out of the Kay Jewelers marketing department.

Thomas Hope brought the Hope Diamond into the clan, where, after his death, it bounced down like a game of expensive pinball through heirs and contested wills and bankruptcies. From the Hope family it went to a jewelry firm, which sold it to a Sergeant Habib on behalf of the sultan of Turkey, who then ran into financial trouble and sold it to yet another jewelry firm. In 1920, Pierre Cartier got his manicured hands on it in Paris.

And we mostly have Cartier to thank for the curse.

By this time, massive diamond mines had been discovered in South Africa. Diamonds had become far more attainable, and not just for the super-rich. Within a few decades, everyone was expected to buy a diamond ring for their fiancée, a tradition that continues to this day — because, you know, diamonds are forever. Gems were becoming mainstream.

Cartier wanted to sell his blue diamond to a member of the emerging wealthy class of the United States, and he knew that to distinguish the diamond in the market and command a higher price, it needed a story. So he marked the diamond up both in cost and with a curse. It wasn't hard. A few spurious newspaper articles had already gotten the ball rolling, and the idea of cursed gems was becoming more widespread due to popular novels such as Wilkie Collins's *The Moonstone* (1868) and Sir Arthur Conan Doyle's *The Sign of the Four* (1890). Cartier also gussied up its presentation, surrounding it with sixteen small white diamonds and creating the look of the Hope Diamond that we know today. Cartier's story of this cursed gem caught the fancy of Evalyn Walsh McLean and her husband, Ned, of Washington, DC. The McLeans bought it for $180,000, or approximately $4.5 million in today's dollars.

During her decades of ownership, Evalyn wore the diamond to countless parties. Sometimes she displayed it on her head in a tiara-like aigrette, sometimes around her neck, and sometimes she even let her dog wear it. She had it blessed by a priest, temporarily pawned it to gather ransom for the doomed Lindbergh baby, and talked freely and amusedly about its curse. When her nine-year-old was struck by a car and killed, the *New York Times* couldn't help but mention the gem in their reporting on the tragedy. Eventually, Ned and Evalyn's relationship ended in divorce, Ned wound up in a sanitarium, and another of their children killed himself. In other words, their lives ended exactly how you'd think the lives of people who brazenly owned a cursed gem would end.

Sometimes she displayed it on her head in a tiara-like aigrette, sometimes around her neck, and sometimes she even let her dog wear it.

After Evalyn's death in 1947, the Hope Diamond was picked up by American jeweler Harry Winston, along with the rest of her jewels, for about a million dollars (roughly $11.5 million today). He toured the Hope Diamond around North America before finally donating it to the Smithsonian National Museum of Natural History in 1958 for a big tax break and the dream of kick-starting a collection of American "crown" jewels. And that's where it is today. From the mantle of the Earth to the capital of the United States.

The Hope Diamond is displayed in the Janet Annenberg Hooker Hall of Geology, Gems, and Minerals at the Smithsonian. It reigns by itself in the center of a room in a rotating case that allows visitors to stand mere inches away . . . if you can buzz-saw your way through all the other museum visitors clustered around the small display case. Many believe the diamond to be the most important and most popular object in the Smithsonian's collection, making it more a lucky charm for the museum than a cursed object. Others think it has cursed the entire country by its prominent inclusion among the nation's treasures.

While it cannot be denied that everyone who has ever owned the Hope Diamond has died, the Hope Diamond can sometimes seem less the direct cause of trouble than a side effect of it. After all, you have to be extremely rich to own it, to the point of taking that wealth and investing it in an ostentatious bauble. That's a level of wealth that comes with its own problems, whether those problems are born of politics or profligacy. In fact, Evalyn Walsh described her own troubles since buying the blue diamond in her 1936 memoir, *Father Struck It Rich*, as "the natural consequence of unearned wealth in undisciplined hands." This was probably a dig at her husband.

It isn't surprising that any gemstone rare enough or large enough to merit its own name also merits its own curse. Maybe it's a subconscious moralizing against greed or perhaps fantasy retribution against the über-rich. Maybe, by ascribing so many stories to it and retelling those stories, those of us who could never afford such a jewel gain a communal ownership of it.

By that logic, by writing this entry I own the Hope Diamond. Hopefully I can retire off that.

Ötzi the Iceman

PLACE OF ORIGIN: ÖTZTAL ALPS, ITALY	**CAUSE OF DEATH:** MURDER
YEAR OF DISCOVERY: 1991	**CURRENT LOCATION:** SOUTH TYROL MUSEUM OF ARCHAEOLOGY, BOLZANO, ITALY
AGE: 5,300 YEARS	**DEATH TOLL:** SEVEN

Otzi the Iceman was a fairy tale of a find: a 5,300-year-old corpse so well preserved that his discoverers could see his tattoos and judge his fashion sense. His relatives, had they not disintegrated into atoms millennia ago, could have easily and conclusively ID'd his body.

In fact, when they found Ötzi, frozen like the Encino Man in the ice of the Ötztal Alps on the border of Austria and Italy, they thought he was an unlucky climber of much more recent vintage. They had no clue they were seeing man, history, and time itself frozen into the snowy flanks of the mountain.

Ötzi was discovered at an elevation of 10,530 feet on September 19, 1991, by a pair of German tourists hiking through the area. After chipping him out, scientists, archeologists, and anthropologists marveled at the discovery . . . and are still marveling and discovering things about him today.

Since being pulled out of the ice and into modern society, Ötzi has had his genome sequenced, his relatives traced, his stomach contents analyzed, his diseases diagnosed (Lyme disease, parasitic gut worms, gallstones, otherwise fine), his age gauged (a respectable forty-five), his body scanned by every imaging modality known to Siemens, and the cold case of his cause of death solved: murder, based on the arrow lodged in

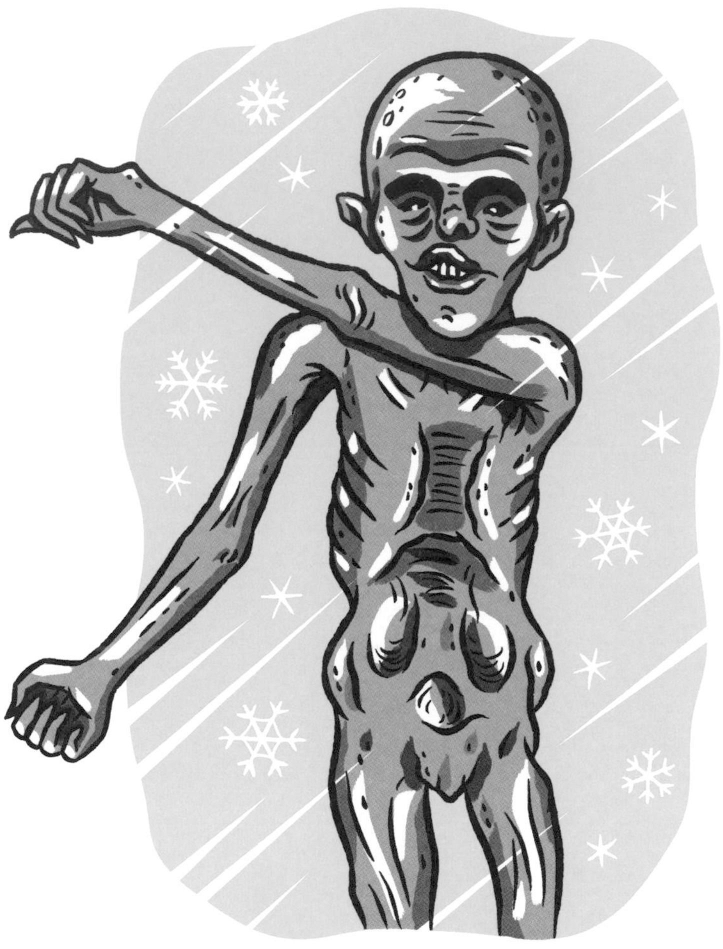

his shoulder from behind and the trauma to his skull. Ötzi also came as a complete set. He was excavated with all of his accessories preserved. His hat and clothes and shoes survived, as did his arrows and axe and dagger and backpack and all the other items that a Copper Age man needed back in the day.

Today, the Iceman looks like a skeleton wrapped in golden-brown leather the quality of expensive shoes. His ankles are crossed, and his arms extend to the right at angles that make him look like he was flash-frozen while doing the floss dance.

And he might just be cursed. Because as lucky a find as he was for anthropology and archeology and about a dozen other -ologies, he proved to be unlucky for many of the people involved with his discovery and study.

The bad luck started in 2004, when one of the German tourists who found him, Helmut Simon, died at age sixty-seven during a blizzard while hiking near where he had first seen the brown lump of historic corpse protruding from the ice. It was almost as if the mountain needed a replacement for Ötzi. An hour after Simon's funeral, Dieter Warnecke, who had been hale enough to lead the rescue team that searched for Simon, died of a heart attack. He was forty-five years old, about the same age the Iceman was when he perished. The next year, an archeologist by the name of Konrad Spindler, who was one of the first experts to analyze Ötzi, died of complications from multiple sclerosis at age fifty-five. His disease was diagnosed not long after his analysis of the Iceman. After that was Rainer Henn, who was a forensic examiner of Ötzi. He died in a car crash at age sixty-four, supposedly while on his way to give a lecture about the naturally formed mummy. Then it was Kurt Fritz, a mountaineer who played a role in Ötzi's original recovery. He died in an avalanche at age fifty-two. Rainer Holz was next on Ötzi's hit list. He was a filmmaker who documented the retrieval of Otzi from the ice. Age at death: forty-seven. Cause: brain tumor.

The last victim – at least thus far – was Tom Loy. He was a molecular biologist who famously identified four different types of blood on the Iceman's clothes and tools, which changed the story of Ötzi's death from one of a lonely hunting accident to that of a fatal skirmish. Loy died at age sixty-three in October 2005 of complications from a blood condition that, according to some sources, was diagnosed soon after his first examination of the Iceman. At the time of his death, Loy was writing a book about Ötzi. Seven deaths in a year: that's a pretty intense body count.

Cursed or not, both Austria and Italy – which shared the mountain Ötzi was found on – wanted the corpse for themselves and fought over him for a while after his discovery. Eventually, it was ascertained that he was found on the Italian side of the mountain. So now you can to head to Italy to test the curse for yourself. Ötzi has been the star of the South Tyrol Museum of Archaeology in Bolzano since 1998.

And I do mean star. The museum dedicates a remarkable three floors to this singular glacier mummy. It even has a lifelike, Hollywood-special-effects-quality reconstruction of Ötzi made of silicone, resin, and human hair, showing what he might have looked like in his less-dead days thousands of years ago.

As for Ötzi himself, he's kept in a cold room and viewable through a window while he continues to outlast everyone else on the planet.

Māori Taonga

PLACE OF ORIGIN:
NEW ZEALAND

TRANSLATION:
"TREASURED ITEMS OF THE MĀORI PEOPLE"

EXAMPLES:
HEIRLOOM ARTIFACTS INCLUDING WEAPONS AND MASKS, BURIAL GROUNDS, AND NATURAL RESOURCES

CURRENT LOCATION:
THROUGHOUT NEW ZEALAND AND IN THE MUSEUM OF NEW ZEALAND TE PAPA TONGAREWA, WELLINGTON, NEW ZEALAND

What do you get when you mix tribal weapons possessed by ghosts and women possessed by tiny humans? Possibly a curse. Definitely a public relations mess. At least, that's what one Wellington, New Zealand, museum discovered in October 2010.

The Museum of New Zealand Te Papa Tongarewa (Te Papa, for short) is the country's national museum. The Māori half of its name translates to "container of treasures." Those treasures, or *taonga*, are a massive array of important artistic and cultural artifacts spanning the history of New Zealand, including those of the indigenous Māori people.

One fateful day that October, the museum was planning a tour of some of the Māori taonga that are kept behind the scenes. Normally these types of events come with the usual stipulations – no touching the artifacts, wear comfortable shoes, no flash photography. However, at Te Papa, the rules stipulated that pregnant women and menstruating women should wait until they are neither of those things before joining the tour.

People were upset by this rule.

The museum tried to push back, explaining that many of these taonga were borrowed from indigenous people and that the museum needed to abide by the rules of those cultures.

People got more upset.

The museum explained that some of these taonga were weapons that had killed men on the battlefield, and if menstruating or pregnant women came into contact with them, a curse would be unleashed. And the museum insurance, presumably, didn't cover that.

People got even more upset. Some escalated to livid.

And that's understandable. Many cultures and religions have rules of varying rigidity regulating what women of childbearing age can and can't do. The Old Testament has stringent rules about menstruation. As does the Koran. Buddhism, Hinduism, all the -isms have something to say on this topic, and most of them amount to the idea that periods are yucky. The Māori prohibition on pregnant and menstruating women around weapons is . . . maybe more complicated than that. But maybe not.

Māori and other Polynesian peoples subscribe to a concept called *tapu*. It's where English gets the word *taboo* from, thanks to eighteenth-century British explorer Captain James Cook who imported it. Tapu means something sacred that should be avoided. To violate tapu is to become cursed, more or less; the gods either directly aim bad juju at you or remove their protection from you, making you susceptible to all manner of natural and supernatural ills. And, obviously, nobody wants to hang out with you.

Anything can be tapu. A lake, a forest, a house, a tool, a weapon, a person, a person's leg. Whatever is tapu needs to be avoided, lest that tapu becomes violated and contaminates whoever violated it. For instance, if your left hand becomes tapu, you're not allowed to feed yourself with it. An opposite force, called *noa*, which is sort of but not really like the idea of a blessing, can counteract tapu.

Still, tapu isn't bad intrinsically. Tapu was often asserted to protect lands from misuse, such as water sources and burial grounds. It can elevate people and objects to a protected status. But violating tapu is bad. Really bad. Every tapu object has the potential to be a cursed object if it's not treated appropriately.

In the case of the Māori taonga on display at Te Papa, many of these items were weapons that had killed people in battle. In Māori culture, when a *toa* – a warrior – dies on the battlefield, his spirit enters the instrument of his destruction. Basically, Te Papa had a bunch of possessed objects in its back rooms. And like many implements associated with death in Māori culture, they are tapu.

Pregnant and menstruating women are also tapu. For instance, pregnant women aren't supposed to give birth inside their homes because doing so would make their homes tapu. They are supposed to do so in purpose-built or specially designated sites.

Another thing about tapu objects is that they can violate each other if they come into contact or close proximity. When that happens, a curse is unleashed that yields all the usual curse results: death, disaster, misfortune. So having a tapu spear in close quarters with a tapu woman would be bad news for the museum and the people who had entrusted those objects to its care.

These beliefs were what the museum was defending. Eventually, after the backlash reached an annoying-enough level, the museum leaders explained that the rule was merely a suggestion, not a prohibition. If a woman wanted to risk unleashing a curse, she could feel free. Whether any pregnant women or women on their periods ignored the suggestion is uncertain. Accounts of the event, which avidly document the situation up to that point, end when the rules were retracted. So we don't know if any tapu were crossed.

But we do know what happened to the museum in subsequent years. In 2015, Te Papa suddenly realized that many items on display had been damaged by visitors touching them. In 2016, fire sprinklers malfunctioned, damaging precious artifacts. Later that year, Te Papa was rocked by an earthquake, damaging both the facility and its holdings. And in 2018, staff discovered that the museum's impressive whale bone collection had contracted a harmful species of mold.

I mean, sure, maybe those incidents are the normal trials and travails of any museum. But who knows? When much of your collection is inextricable from a system like tapu, the risks of violating it are always there.

The Tomb of Tutankhamen

LOCATION:	YEAR OF DISCOVERY:
VALLEY OF THE KINGS, LUXOR, EGYPT	1922
SIGNIFICANCE:	AGE:
BURIAL SITE OF THE FAMOUS CHILD PHARAOH	3,300 YEARS
	NUMBER OF ITEMS:
	MORE THAN 5,000

When King Tut's tomb unleashed its ancient curse across the desert sands of Egypt and into the modern world, it wasn't in the form of Biblical plagues or killer mummies or natural disasters. It came in the form of . . . a shaving accident.

Tutankhamen was an Eighteenth Dynasty pharaoh from the early 1300s BCE. Perhaps the most interesting thing about his reign is that he was nine years old when he ascended the throne. Perhaps the second most interesting thing about his reign is that it ended ten years later with his death, the cause of which has been lost to history. But that's okay, because we have his mummy.

In 1922, his preserved body was pulled from its ancient sandy slumber within a surprisingly intact tomb in the well-looted Valley of the Kings. We all know him by his nickname, King Tut, and he made ancient Egypt cool again in the Western world.

The tomb of Tutankhamen was discovered by British archeologist Howard Carter. But it took some time. He probed the sands from 1917 to 1922, looking for the boy king. In November 1922, his last season before his funding was due to be pulled by his patron, George Herbert, the Fifth Earl of Carnarvon, one of his Egyptian crew tripped over a rock that turned out to be the first in a series of sixteen steps buried under the sand. After excavating a doorway at the bottom of those stairs, Carter dutifully ordered that everything be reburied. Then he called up the earl and said, "I found the kid's tomb. Let's crack it open together." (To paraphrase.)

Later that month, Carter and Lord Carnarvon did exactly that, clearing the way to the door, which they found to bear the symbols of King Tut as well as evidence of a breach by possible grave robbers. Nevertheless, days of digging later, Carter's candle illuminated through a hole in the door an antechamber full of archeological treasures . . . and actual treasure, since much of it was gold. Most exciting, they saw another door behind it, this one with the seals intact.

Next came the slow, steady work of cataloguing the artifacts on their way to the sealed door and its promise of a dead boy king. It took about seven weeks. Meanwhile, headlines around the world touted the find and tourists crowded the site, watching as these treasures were carted to a nearby empty tomb for documentation. Then, just as the antechamber was cleared, the tomb was closed for the season. The world would have to wait a little longer to see if the tomb still held its royal mummy.

Lord Carnarvon would never find out. During the break, while in Aswan in southern Egypt, he was bit by a mosquito, and then he nicked the bite while shaving. He contracted blood poisoning and died shortly thereafter. His death gave

the curse story life. It took off partly because there was already a template in place thanks to previously discovered cursed Egyptian funeral objects (namely, the Unlucky Mummy – see page 44), but also because Carnarvon had sold exclusive press rights to the dig to the *Times* of London, leaving all other media outside the ropes with the tourists. But with Carnarvon dead, they didn't need access anymore. They had a whole new angle on the King Tut story: the curse of the pharaohs.

The story was further helped along by people like Sir Arthur Conan Doyle, who posited that nature spirits called elementals (my dear Watson) that guarded the tomb must have taken vengeance upon Carnarvon for disturbing it. Another author, Marie Corelli, attested that she owned a rare Egyptian book that explained that royal tombs contain secret poisons for defilers. People added apocryphal events to the timeline, for instance, that a cobra – a symbol of the pharaohs – ate

His suicide note stated, "I can't stand any more horrors."

Carnarvon's canary on the day he opened the tomb. That his dog howled and died on the same day that he did. That a clay tablet with a curse was found in the tomb and then destroyed by Carter and Carnarvon so that the workers wouldn't see it and be scared away. That when Tut was unwrapped, he bore a matching facial wound to Carnarvon's lethal shaving one.

Meanwhile, Carter kept digging. He reached the burial chamber in early 1923, where he found King Tut's body and more than 5,000 other items, including a gold coffin and

Tut's iconic gold mask. But overshadowing this discovery that reinvigorated Egyptian archeology were all the people connected to the dig who died after Carnarvon. The lists reads like the lyrics to Jim Carroll's "People Who Died."

After Carnarvon, there was railroad magnate George Jay Gould, who visited the freshly opened tomb and died of pneumonia shortly thereafter. Egyptian aristocrat Ali Kamel Fahmy Bey, another early tomb visitor, was shot by his wife that same year. Still in 1923, Carnarvon's half-brother Aubrey Herbert died from what some say was blood poisoning. In 1924, Archibald Douglas Reid, a radiologist who x-rayed King Tut's sarcophagus, died from a mysterious illness, and Sir Lee Stack, Governor-General of Sudan and one of the first people to visit the tomb, was assassinated in Cairo. In 1926, French Egyptologist Georges Bénédite perished after taking a fall outside the tomb. Arthur Mace, a member of Carter's team, suffered ill health after twenty years in the field and had to retire from Egypt. He died in 1928, some say from arsenic poisoning.

Jumping to 1929, another of Carnarvon's half-brothers, Mervyn Herbert, succumbed to pneumonia. That same year Captain Richard Bethell, who worked for both Carnarvon and Carter in various roles, died in bed under suspicious circumstances. Months later, his father threw himself out the window of his seventh-floor apartment. His suicide note stated, "I can't stand any more horrors."

All these people were somehow connected to the discovery of King Tut, and they all died within seven years. But the carnage didn't stop there. The list of people claimed to be cursed by King Tut grew exponentially over the decades. Anybody who visited the tomb, wrote about it, transferred artifacts from it, or was related to someone who did those things was rewarded with the word *curse* in their obituary.

But what of Howard Carter? The guy without whom King Tut might still be twice buried? He lived for almost two decades after opening the tomb, dying at age sixty-four of Hodgkin's disease in London. His grave bears an inscription taken from the Wishing Cup of King Tut, a chalice found in the tomb: "May your spirit live, may you spend millions of years, you who love Thebes, sitting with your face to the north wind, your eyes beholding happiness."

In the end, the curse of King Tut's tomb has thrived because it makes sense as a story. What do you expect to happen when you defile the ancient dead and dump out the afterlife-bound treasures of a death-and-eternity-obsessed culture? If anything is cursed in the history of the world, the Egyptian tomb of a royal must be.

Historically, Tut has been on display in his tomb for anyone to see, while many of the treasures of his afterlife have been exhibited at the Egyptian Museum in Cairo, as well as at museums around the world in traveling shows that spread the curse across the planet.

However, as of the writing of this book and after almost a decade of stop-and-start-construction, Egypt is putting the finishing touches on its new Grand Egyptian Museum in Cairo. It's touted as one of the largest museums in the world. The museum will reunite all 5,000-plus artifacts from King Tut's tomb in one massive exhibit, including the body of the boy king himself.

If anything's worth risking a curse, it might be a visit to this museum.

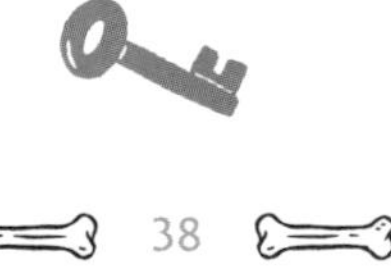

A Curse Is Forever

In addition to the Hope Diamond, other cursed gemstones include the Koh-i-Noor diamond, the Black Prince's Ruby, the Regent Diamond, the Sancy yellow diamond, the Delhi Purple Sapphire, the Star of India sapphire, and the Black Orlov diamond. Though the stones are different, their stories are similar.

They usually originate in the gem-fertile earth of India, where they were placed in and plucked from the eye sockets of holy idols. European imperialism or mercantilism brought them to the Western world, where they adorned the spiky hats of royalty. Some eventually immigrated to America, bought by the kings and queens of capitalism. Some shrank over the centuries as gem cutters carved them down to satisfy personal tastes or as gem-cutting technology advanced. Eventually, many ended up in museums, trapped under glass like they were once trapped under the Earth's mantle.

You can see the Koh-i-Noor and the Black Prince's Ruby in the Tower of London with the rest of the British crown jewels. The Regent and the Sancy diamonds are at the Louvre. Marie Antoinette wore both before she lost a place to hang a necklace. The Delhi Purple Sapphire, which is technically an amethyst, is at London's Natural History Museum. The Star of India is at the American Museum of Natural History in New York. It was stolen in 1964 but was found and returned three months later. The Black Orlov is currently in a private collection.

Muramasa Swords

PLACE OF ORIGIN:
KUWANA, JAPAN

CREATED BY:
SENGO MURAMASA

AGE:
~500 YEARS

CURRENT WHEREABOUTS:
MUSEUMS AND PRIVATE COLLECTIONS THROUGHOUT JAPAN

Cursed weapons have a big advantage over other cursed objects: they can do the dirty work of the curse themselves rather than waiting for something else to harm the curse victim – say, a bus or cancer or an iceberg. And it's inarguable by even the most immovable skeptic of the paranormal that anybody at the bad end of a weapon is, if not cursed, at the very least unlucky.

Perhaps the most famous examples of cursed weapons – that is, ones not appearing in a fantasy book or video game – are the swords of Sengo Muramasa, a man whose story is so wrapped in legend that it's difficult to parse what parts are true and what parts are lore.

Muramasa was an infamous sixteenth-century Japanese swordsmith. Japan had always taken its swords seriously, but Muramasa elevated the art of crafting these lethal weapons.

The quality of his blades was higher, the metal stronger, the edges sharper. The swords seemed deadlier than most – so deadly that people couldn't believe that they were the products of mere heating and hammering, folding and sharpening like every other sword stabbing the scabbards of Japan's warriors. People needed a better explanation. A supernatural one.

So stories circulated that Muramasa was a violent madman who transferred his insanity and rage right into his metal blades. Or that he made an infernal pact with dark forces to create those superhuman pointy things. However it happened, the *katana* and *wakizashi* forged by Muramasa demanded blood, and once they were unsheathed, they would not return to their scabbards until they were shiny and slick with it, sending their wielders into a frothy mania of violence. If the warrior could find nobody to slice open and satisfy the bloodlust of the sword, he would have to impale himself on his own blade. Basically, Muramasa's swords were lethal both to their victims and to those who wielded them. Deadly at both ends, you could say.

It is said that at one point Muramasa tested one of his swords against that of Japan's most famous swordsmith, Masamune. Both men stuck their blades into a fast-moving stream. Masamune's blade split every leaf that the current pushed its way while sparing the fish; Muramasa's blade sliced both plants and fish, proving its lack of discrimination when it came to violence. If the story sounds more like a parable than a historical event, that's because it is. Masamune lived hundreds of years before Muramasa.

What truly cemented Muramasa swords as cursed in the imagination of the general public of Japan, though, is a different story. According to this one, the blades were banned by Shogun Ieyasu Tokugawa because he came to believe that they were a curse on his family. Ieyasu was the founder of the Tokugawa shogunate, a hereditary military dictatorship that ruled Japan for a good 250 years beginning in the early seventeenth century. Although we don't know exactly when Muramasa started making swords, we do know that his blades were still around in seventeenth-century Japan. In fact, the master swordsmith had passed down his technique to apprentices and founded a school dedicated to sword-making that lasted for two centuries, extending his deadly reach as a maniac sword maker through time.

So why did Ieyasu believe that the demented swordsmith's blades were cursed? Because numerous members of his family were killed by them. Ieyasu's grandfather was cut in two by one wielded by his retainer, Ieyasu's father was killed by one (possibly also wielded by a retainer), and, to round out the generational bad luck, Ieyasu's son was beheaded by one as part of seppuku, a ritual suicide. Ieyasu himself had been harmed by one of the swords as a child. According to the lore, Ieyasu outlawed Muramasa swords, and any person found with one was sentenced to death. Legend has it that a magistrate of Nagasaki, Takanak Ume, was found to have twenty-four of these blades in his collection. Seppuku for him.

However, it's more likely that Ieyasu appreciated Muramasa swords. He used them. His samurai were equipped with them. Given that he was surrounded by them, it makes sense that he knew a lot of victims of these weapons. But the myth of his family's curse, plus other references to Muramasa blades as evil or demonic, persisted in transmogrifying these terrifying killing tools into . . . much more terrifying killing tools.

And although the story of Ieyasu's ban is probably not true, it did become meaningful. Over the centuries, the curse story transformed into a political parable that Muramasa swords were cursed against the shogunate system. This idea was promoted by anti-Tokugawa activists who actively sought out Muramasa blades to use as symbols against the shogunate they were looking to unseat. Apparently it worked; the Tokugawa shogunate established by Ieyasu was Japan's last.

Today, more than half a millennium later, Muramasa swords are still around and are still, presumably, lethal. Many are held in private collections. Some are displayed at museums, including the Tokyo National Museum and the Japanese Sword Museum, also in the capital. Every once in a while, they travel the world as part of exhibitions. In 2017, Japan's prime minister Shinzo Abe gave a Muramasa dagger to Russian president Vladimir Putin.

These days, it can be difficult to tell a real Muramasa from a fake, despite the distinctness of their features. Authentic Muramasas have a recognizable wave-shaped pattern (called the *hamon*) that is mirrored on both sides of the blade. The part of the blade embedded in the hilt (the *tang*) is uniquely formed in what's been termed a "fish belly" shape. However, the swords were in such demand by anti-shogunate activists that many fakes were made. In addition, some say that even real Muramasa blades were altered to disguise them during Ieyasu's supposed ban.

The best way to tell whether a sword is a Muramasa product or not, is, of course, to unsheathe one and see if it demands blood.

The Unlucky Mummy

PLACE OF ORIGIN: DAYR EL BAHREE, EGYPT	**PURPOSE:** COFFIN LID OF A PRIESTESS OF AMEN-RA
YEAR OF DISCOVERY: 1868	**CURRENT LOCATION:** BRITISH MUSEUM, LONDON, ENGLAND
AGE: 3,000 YEARS	

We know that an iceberg took out the *Titanic*. We know that the assassination of Archduke Franz Ferdinand of Austria kicked off World War I. But what if I told you that both of these horrible hash marks of human history were caused by a single cursed object? One looted from an Egyptian tomb? One that predates the discovery of King Tut's tomb by decades and, in fact, provided a template for the curse stories that swirl around that famous boy king's grave to this day (see page 33)?

Cursed mummies are common in the lore. Take the mummy of Nesmin, whose British buyer was trampled to death by an elephant. Or Khentika Ikhekhi, a vizier whose tomb contains a warning that he will rise and strangle anybody who defiles it. But the mummy whose curse is the subject of this entry is weirder than most cursed mummies. Because it's not actually a mummy. It's a . . . lid. Granted, that lid belongs to the coffin of a mummified priestess, but it's still a lid. *Mummy board* is the technical term. And the name of this mummy board is the Unlucky Mummy. Seriously. That's the exact name that appears in the British Museum catalog.

The Unlucky Mummy is about five feet long and is shaped and painted like the woman it once covered. She's depicted with dark hair that falls down to her shoulders. Her arms are crossed, with her hands held out flat like she's making butterfly wings with them. She's covered in colorful patterns and repeating images of people and gods and insects and animals. She doesn't look malevolent. She looks mildly peaceful with

her lot in death. She is an image of a priestess of Amen-Ra who lived about three thousand years ago, during the Twenty-first Dynasty of Egypt. But the mummy priestess that this board shaded in death has long since disappeared to history.

Even without counting a massive ocean liner and a world war, this ancient Egyptian artifact with a name like a children's picture book title is supposed to have inflicted death and disaster upon an uncounted number of British citizens, starting with the group of four Oxford graduates who picked it up in 1868 during a trip to Dayr el Bahree in Egypt. Two are said to have died on the trip. A third, Thomas Douglas Murray, had his arm amputated after accidentally shooting himself while quail hunting in Cairo. The fourth, Arthur Wheeler, was the only member of the party to make it back unscathed . . . until he lost his fortune, twice. Wheeler eventually became the sole owner of the mummy board. After it made it to England, a photographer died after photographing it, as did a porter after carrying it, and a translator of the board's hieroglyphs shot himself after trying to solve its secrets.

The one-armed Murray is likely the original source of most of these claims. Murray made frequent visits to Egypt in the 1860s and was a member of the Ghost Club, a spiritualist society whose members would weave ghost stories into their pipe smoke. He shared the tale of the cursed lid with his fellow members on multiple occasions, and eventually the story made it into the newspapers with big bold headlines. He lived to the age of seventy, telling paranormal stories and helping introduce the Western world to the Pekingese dog breed.

Eventually, the Unlucky Mummy arrived at the most prestigious place for an ancient Egyptian artifact in England – the British Museum. Once there, in the public eye, its bloody provenance really got people talking, especially after a journalist named Bertram Fletcher Robinson wrote a front-page article on the board in the *Daily Express* in 1904, calling the painted piece of wood and plaster the "Priestess of Death." It was a much better moniker than Unlucky Mummy, but the nickname didn't stick. For his trouble, Robinson died three years after writing about the mummy board.

Deaths were continuously attributed to the Unlucky Mummy. For a while, you couldn't die in England without your survivors wondering if your trip to the British Museum had caused it. And those rumors gradually expanded so that anything unfortunate happening anywhere in England was traced to the Unlucky Mummy . . . like the voyage of the *Titanic*, which picked up its doomed passengers in Southampton.

There are a few stories about the *Titanic* transporting a secret mummy in its hold. In the version featuring the Unlucky Mummy, it's there because the British Museum had tired of losing so many staff and visitors to the curse and got rid of the item by selling it to a museum or rich collector in America. Yet, somehow, the Unlucky Mummy was lucky enough to survive the sinking of the *Titanic*. The cursed object supposedly arrived in America in 1912, where it immediately began causing havoc and was therefore returned to its sender two years later. The ship that returned it was the RMS *Empress of Ireland*, which also sank, after colliding with the SS *Storstad* in the Saint Lawrence River in Quebec, killing more than one thousand people.

But three ships full of the wet dead can't hold a prayer candle to the casualties of World War I. The Unlucky Mummy was recovered again out of the Canadian drink, and this time it was sold to a German who presented it to Kaiser Wilhelm II, the last German emperor. Then a globe-encompassing war ensued, which had never happened in the history of the planet until the Unlucky Mummy came to Britain.

However, none of these globe-trotting and seafaring tales are true. During all the time when the Unlucky Mummy was supposed to be in ship holds, at the bottom of oceans and rivers, and in Germany, this cursed object in fact stayed dry and behind glass at the British Museum. It only left English soil a few times, and that was after 1990, when it joined exhibitions in countries that had little regard for the damage it was rumored to cause.

Today, the Unlucky Mummy is still on display in the British Museum, among all the Egyptian treasures that make it one of the best collections of Egyptian antiquities in the world. In fact, it's surrounded by many complete mummy coffins and actual mummies and other spooky artifacts that seem much more worthy of being cursed.

Heck, it's even easy to miss. You can walk through the entire exhibit, taking pictures of everything that seems eye-catching or noteworthy . . . and still completely miss her amid all the other mummy boards in the vast collection.

Which is fine. Because, hopefully, that means she'll miss you, too.

The Ring of Silvianus

PLACE OF ORIGIN:
SILCHESTER, HAMPSHIRE, ENGLAND

YEAR OF DISCOVERY:
1785

AGE:
1,700 YEARS

CURRENT LOCATION:
THE VYNE, SHERBORNE ST. JOHN, ENGLAND

If you're a farmer in Great Britain, you're used to turning up museum-quality stuff when you plough through the dirt. Maybe a coin from when the Roman Empire ruled the land. Or a buckle dropped by a questing knight during the medieval period. Perhaps a small Celtic blade used in some dark and mysterious druid ceremony. After all, you're planting crops atop a small island whose rich history spans millennia.

In 1785, while working in his fields in Silchester, Hampshire, a farmer did just this and found a gold ring, one that would turn out to be a cursed gold ring — a cursed gold ring that would inspire the ultimate cursed gold ring.

The artifact was a large signet ring bearing the concave image of the goddess Venus on its bezel. The band had ten subtle facets, like a worn lug nut. Engraved into the outside of the band were letters spelling out the Latin phrase "SENICIANE VIVAS IIN DE" backward, so that when pressed into wax the phrase could be read from left to right as, "Senicianus live well in God." Although the phrase was misspelled, like whoever had it engraved was in a hurry. Turns out, he might have been running from a curse.

It was a good find for the British farmer, though. Made of gold and dating back to the fourth century, the ring was worth some money and held historic interest. But that's as far as it went for a time. Again, Great Britain is nubby with buried artifacts. The farmer sold the ring to the Chute family, who were wealthy and politically connected and lived in Hampshire at a sixteenth century estate called the Vyne. The ring was added to the family's large collection of antiquities and probably would have been forgotten about had another artifact not been unearthed in the next century about eighty miles from the farmer's field.

In Gloucestershire are the ruins of a Roman temple dedicated to the god Nodens. He's in charge of healing, hunting, and the sea. (Most ancient gods are multitaskers.) The land where the ruins are located is officially called Lydney Camp, although it was also known as Dwarf's Hill in honor of the type of supernatural creatures that were thought to inhabit the area after the Romans left.

Found in those ruins in the nineteenth century was a small, thin lead tablet with a curse inscribed on it. Thousands of these lead or stone curse tablets (called *defixiones*) have been found across Europe, such as the seventh-century defixio found in Cyprus bearing the message: "May your penis hurt when you make love." And the Porcellus defixio, which features the image of a snake-haired demon above a mummified curse victim. Defixiones are a lot of fun.

On the defixio found on Dwarf's Hill, the following curse was inscribed:

For the god Nodens. Silvianus has lost a ring and has donated one half its worth to Nodens. Among those named Senicianus permit no good health until it is returned to the temple of Nodens.

That's right. A ring engraved with the name Senicianus was found eighty miles away from a tablet calling down a curse upon a man named Senicianus who had stolen a ring. And in those days, the name Senicianus was no John Smith.

In 1888, a century after the ring was found, Chaloner William Chute, the heir to the Vyne estate, wrote about the connection between the lead tablet and the ring in his family's possession in his book *A History of the Vyne in Hampshire*. He hypothesized that Senicianus stole the ring from Silvianus while both were visiting Nodens's temple. There were a lot of opportunities for such thievery at the temple, where pilgrims would stay overnight and dip into healing baths. It's the ancient Roman equivalent of somebody stealing your phone from your locker at the gym.

But if the ring had belonged to Silvianus, why was it engraved with Senicianus's name? Perhaps Senicianus, knowing how easy it is to curse somebody while at a temple dedicated to a god, quickly had his own name engraved on the ring, as well as an anti-curse of sorts. Such a rush job could explain the misspelling. Or maybe the ring originally belonged to Senicianus and he lost it to Silvianus in a wager but kept it anyway. Whether Silvianus's defixio worked is a part of the story we'll never know . . . unless somebody digs up yet another artifact to shed more light on this 1,700-year-old drama.

But the story doesn't end there. In fact, it gets even stranger — and relevant to anybody who is a fan of fantasy literature. In 1929, an archaeologist named Sir Mortimer Wheeler was researching the ring and the tablet while excavating Dwarf's Hill when he inadvertently inspired another story, one that eventually became one of the most popular works of literature of the twentieth century.

Wheeler needed help researching the etymology of the god name-checked in the curse, Nodens. He called up an expert in Anglo-Saxon, a well-respected professor at the prestigious

Oxford University: John Ronald Reuel Tolkien. Known to history as J. R. R. Tolkien.

And then, not long after that encounter, J. R. R. Tolkien published his genre-defining fantasy novel, *The Hobbit*, which tells the story of an engraved gold ring that was made by dwarves and cursed. That ring is lost and found, and its finder is chased by the previous owner, who knows the name of the thief: Bagginses.

We don't have proof that the Ring of Silvianus directly inspired the famous fantasist, nor do we have watertight evidence that the ring found in the Silchester field is the same ring that's mentioned on the curse tablet from the Roman temple ruins. But the most improbable circumstances and seemingly coincidental connections can sometimes turn out to be the true story. And in the absence of proof either way, isn't it more fun to believe?

Today, you can see the ring for yourself. The Vyne is a historic site, open to the public, and dedicates an entire room to the piece. It's called the Ring Room. In it is the shiny Ring of Silvianus on display beside a copy of the curse tablet. The original defixio can be viewed at the museum in Lydney Camp.

The ring and the copy of the curse tablet are displayed with, of course, a first edition of J. R. R. Tolkien's *The Hobbit*.

Cursed in the Graveyard

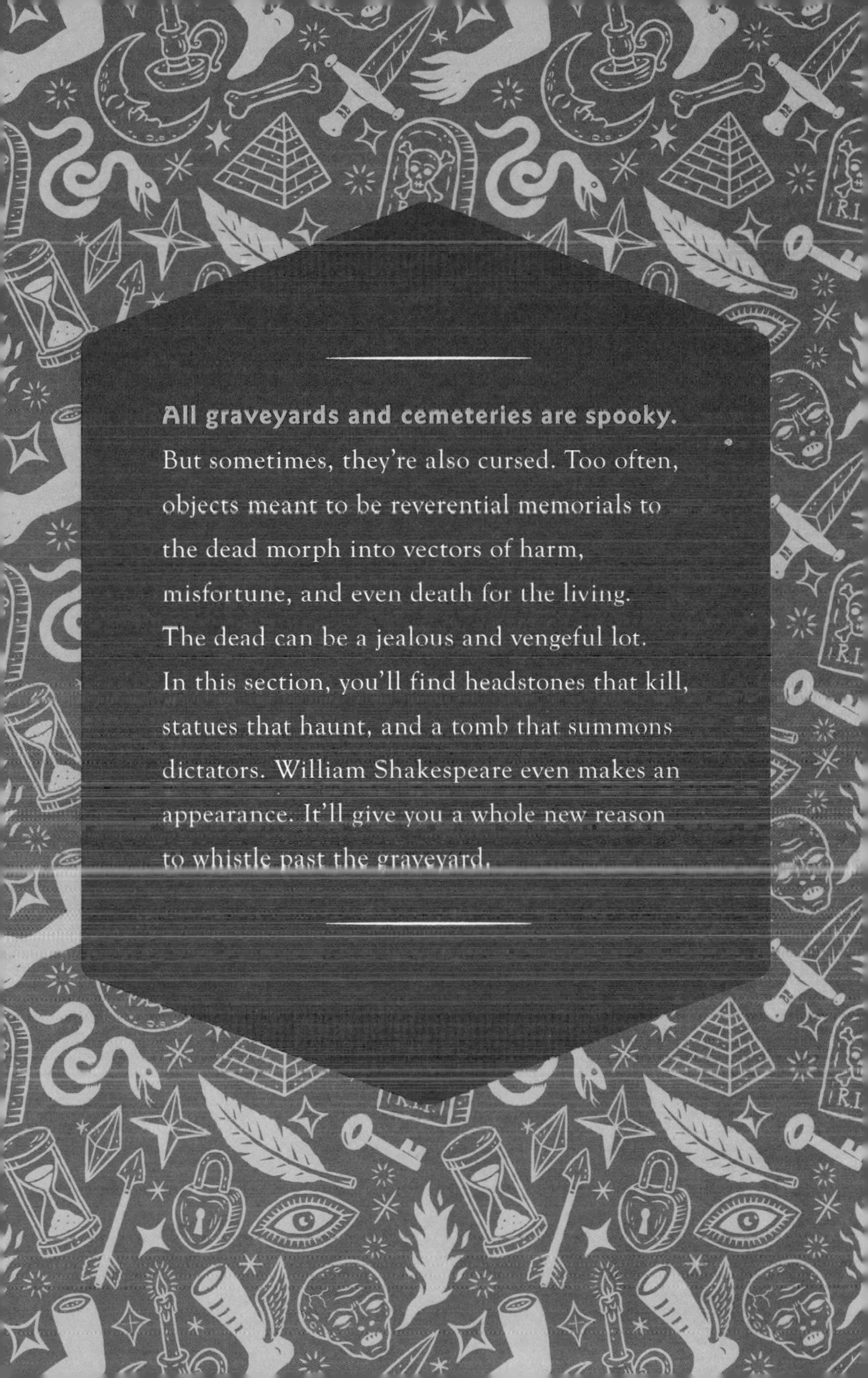

All graveyards and cemeteries are spooky. But sometimes, they're also cursed. Too often, objects meant to be reverential memorials to the dead morph into vectors of harm, misfortune, and even death for the living. The dead can be a jealous and vengeful lot. In this section, you'll find headstones that kill, statues that haunt, and a tomb that summons dictators. William Shakespeare even makes an appearance. It'll give you a whole new reason to whistle past the graveyard.

The Black Aggie

PLACE OF ORIGIN: DRUID RIDGE CEMETERY, PIKESVILLE, MARYLAND	**YEAR OF INSTALLATION:** 1925
SCULPTOR: EDWARD PAUSCH	**CURRENT LOCATION:** HOWARD T. MARKEY NATIONAL COURTS BUILDING, WASHINGTON, DC
CREATED FOR: GENERAL FELIX AGNUS	

When a cemetery has a name like Druid Ridge, you expect it to have a creepy grave statue or two. And Druid Ridge Cemetery in Pikesville, Maryland, has a doozy of one. Or, rather, it did. Today, if you walk its pleasant, winding paths, you'll eventually come across an empty, chair-like pedestal with the name Agnus engraved into its base.

This is the abandoned throne of the Black Aggie, a cursed funerary sculpture with a strange past and an almost stranger present. The Black Aggie is a six-foot-tall shrouded figure in bronze. She sits on a stone. Her eyes are closed. Her hand lifts to rest beneath her chin. She is, in a word, creepy. And the legends that surround her are even more so.

They say her eyes glow red at night and that if you look into them, you'll go blind. They say that if a pregnant woman walks through her shadow, that woman will miscarry. They

say that at night, the spirits of the cemetery gather around her. They say that if you sit on her lap, you will die. They say if you stay overnight with her, you will die.

According to the most specific story told about the Black Aggie, her arm went missing in 1962. It was found in the car of a local sheet metal worker, who claimed that the statue had ripped it off herself one night and handed it to him. It is an outrageous story, but five minutes in the presence of the statue at night might make you inclined to believe it.

There is a good reason for this statue to be cursed. The Black Aggie is an unsanctioned knockoff of a genuine work of funerary art, the Adams Memorial, which was made to memorialize a woman who killed herself.

Henry Adams, of the influential Adams family that gave us two presidents, returned home one day in December 1885 to find his wife of more than a decade, Marian "Clover" Adams, dead on the floor. She had ingested potassium cyanide, a chemical that she normally used to develop her photography. Nobody knows why she killed herself. If there was a suicide note left behind, her husband destroyed it.

Adams hired famed Irish-born American sculptor Augustus Saint-Gaudens to create a work of art to memorialize his wife that could be placed above her (and eventually his) grave in Rock Creek Cemetery in Washington, DC. The sculpture didn't have a name, but folks who saw it called it *Grief* and proclaimed it to be one of the most profound expressions of mourning and loss in the funerary art genre. It was immediately famous. Immediately touristed. And, shortly before Saint-Gaudens's death in 1907, ripped off.

The copycat was the celebrated sculptor Edward Pausch, who created a replica of the Adams Memorial for General

Felix Agnus, a French-born Civil War veteran and newspaper publisher in Baltimore. Agnus proudly erected the statue on his family plot in Druid Ridge Cemetery in Maryland, about thirty-five miles from the place where the Adams Memorial loomed. The widow of Saint-Gaudens, Augusta, was outraged by the unauthorized copy of her husband's statue and threatened legal action. But Agnus refused to remove the statue.

In 1925, Agnus was buried under his bootleg sculpture. But instead of becoming a renowned work of art like its inspiration, the Black Aggie — as it was nicknamed — became the dark shadow of the Adams Memorial. The Jekyll to its Hyde. She became one of Maryland's most prominent cursed objects.

Things got so bad at Druid Ridge Cemetery, what with the attention and the scary stories and the people who would trespass at night to test their mettle against the statue, that, in 1967, the Black Aggie was removed from the cemetery. The Agnus family donated it to the Smithsonian, the curators of which didn't want to display the knockoff. Instead, the Black Aggie was shoved in a basement, which ensured that nobody could stare at her glowing eyes or walk through her deadly shadow. Three years later, the museum received an authorized casting of the original Adams Memorial, which they gave a place of honor in the museum proper, and which still sits there today. While the official casting of the Adams Memorial lorded itself in a gallery, the illegal knockoff Black Aggie moldered in the underworld of the museum archives. In 1987, the General Services Administration (GSA) asked for the statue because they thought she would make a great garden gnome.

The GSA installed the statue in the courtyard of the Howard T. Markey National Courts Building on Lafayette Square at 717 Madison Place NW. If you visit the building during business hours, you can walk right up to the more-than-a-century-old statue that countless Baltimore teenagers and college students spent their youth swapping stories about and sneaking up to at night. And let me tell you – I know she's an unauthorized copy with a sketchy past, but, man, is that statue striking. Even without glowing eyes.

Interestingly, the courthouse is around the corner from the White House. You can almost see it from the statue, and you can definitely see it a dozen steps away from the statue. And that means it's close to another site. An extremely important site. One that jumpstarted the weird chain of events that yielded this cursed statue.

About five hundred feet from where the Black Aggie sits is the former site of the house where Clover Adams killed herself. The structure was razed to make way for the Hay-Adams Hotel, which is still there today – and which, some say, is haunted by the specter of Clover herself.

The Björketorp Runestone

TYPE OF STONE:	AGE:
MENHIR	1,500 YEARS
TYPE OF RUNES:	CURRENT LOCATION:
PROTO-NORSE	BLEKINGE, SWEDEN
HEIGHT:	POSSIBLE FUNCTIONS:
FOURTEEN FEET	GRAVE, CENOTAPH, SHRINE, BORDER MARKER

The Björketorp Runestone in Sweden is one of the tallest runestones in the world, and judging by the ancient curse inscribed in an ancient language on its ancient flanks, it's not taking crap from anyone. Vikings, you know?

The Nordic countries have their share of cursed runestones. For instance, the Glavendrup Stone in Denmark threatens to turn anyone who disrespects the stone into a warlock (alternately translated as an outcast). The Tryggevælde Runestone, also in Denmark, and the Saleby Runestone in Sweden feature similar curses. But the curses engraved into these stones are gentle warnings compared to the dramatic curse that is carved into the Björketorp Runestone.

The Björketorp Runestone is located in the county of Blekinge in the southeast corner of Sweden, right on the coast of the Baltic Sea. It's in an old burial ground in a forest full of tall, freestanding stones called *menhirs*. The site dates to the Iron Age, sometime in the sixth or seventh century. Some of these menhirs are arranged in circles. One of those circles is composed of three tall stones (so, also technically a triangle), one of which is the Björketorp Runestone. You can tell which one because it bears Proto-Norse runes from proto-Vikings. (Proto-Norse would evolve into Old Norse, which was the language of the Vikings.)

It's about fourteen feet tall, almost a tree of a stone, and is shaped kind of like a large upright bass, with a long, thin neck and a bulbous bottom. On the back is a short phrase in ancient angular markings that have been weathered almost to invisibility, but which are legible thanks to dutiful preservation with regularly applied red paint: "I predict perdition." That phrase by itself may or may not be twistable into a curse depending on how you translate it and in what context it's said. But the stone's cursed status is cemented by the message on the front, which goes into detail on the predicted perdition. It reads:

> I, master of the runes, conceal here runes of power. Incessantly plagued by maleficence, doomed to insidious death is he who breaks this monument. I prophesy destruction.

Or something like that. It depends on the translator. Regardless, it's a pretty intense curse and, unlike other runestones, whose curses are tacked onto the end of more benign inscriptions, the curse is the full content of the Björketorp stone. Fortunately, insidious death and a plague of maleficence only come into play if you break the monument.

The only story that I could find of someone actually trying to do just that is vague enough to sound like legend but nonetheless is worth telling. At some point in the stone's history a farmer was trying to clear the surrounding land so that he could do his farmer thing. He piled wood around the runestone so that he could light the wood, heat the runestone, and then pour cold water on the stone, thinking that the abrupt change in temperature would crack it into pieces for easier removal. The farmer lit the fire, but then a strange wind blew through the burial ground, simultaneously dousing the blaze around the runestone and fanning the flames in the farmer's direction, burning him alive and/or dead. Insidious death and maleficence, indeed.

A handful of theories attempt to explain what this stone actually is, besides a prompt for imaginative stories of burning death and anti-agriculturism. The first is that it's a gravestone and that some proto-Viking is buried beneath it. Makes sense. It's in a burial ground, after all. However, in 1914, the area around the stone was excavated, and no remains were found, which seems to rule out this theory.

The second theory is that it's a cenotaph — a grave marker memorializing a dead person whose remains are elsewhere, maybe lost at sea or rotting on a foreign battlefield or buried far from home. Makes sense. It's in a burial ground with no bodies under it.

The third theory is that it's a shrine dedicated to the All-father Odin. Also makes sense. Vikings, you know?

The final theory is that it's a mere border marker between the ancient Swedes and their neighbors the ancient Danes. I hope that one's not true — it's boring.

All of these theories put the stone's curse in different contexts. Depending on which is true, the runestone could be protecting the earthly remains or memory of a dead person, protecting against blasphemy against the gods, or protecting the sanctity of borders.

Or the inscription could have been a common phrase. A proto-meme, perhaps. I say this because, about thirty-five miles west of the Björketorp Runestone, another stone was found with almost the exact same curse in the exact same ancient runic language engraved on its surface: the Stentoften Runestone. The Stentoften Runestone doesn't break any records in height, and is more oblong in shape, but its connection to the Björketorp Runestone is clear. It was discovered by a priest in 1823. He found it facedown and surrounded by five other stones in the shape of a pentagram, an arrangement which might have been intended to ward off evil beings like trolls. These days, the Stentoften Runestone can also be found in Blekinge county, at a church in Sölvesborg – a holy house surrounding a hellish curse.

There are a lot of runestones around the world in a lot of different languages. But few are as surly as the Björketorp Runestone, which is a giant middle finger of a cursed object jutting out of the ground in a forest. That's Vikings for you.

The Tomb of Timur

CURRENT LOCATION:	AGE:
SAMARKAND, UZBEKISTAN	~650 YEARS
SIGNIFICANCE:	**ALSO KNOWN AS:**
BURIAL SITE OF TIMUR, THE LEGENDARY CONQUEROR	GUR-E-AMIR (TOMB OF THE KING)

Timur was the scourge of central Asia during the late fourteenth century. In three and a half decades, he conquered the region, massacring entire populations, destroying cities, and constructing towers from the skulls of his victims.

He also might have sicced Adolf Hitler on Russia six hundred years later by cursing his own tomb. We'll get to that.

Timur was born around 1336 in Transoxiana, now modern-day Uzbekistan. He was the son of Taragay, the leader of one of central Asia's many tribes, and lived in a tumultuous time, with those tribes fighting and jockeying for power. Timur was particularly ambitious and bloodthirsty, and after starting his career as a mercenary solider, he began forming alliances, finding a following, and eventually became the ultimate military force in the land.

He positioned himself as a descendant of Genghis Khan and then tried to outdo the Mongol leader in sheer ruthlessness and ambition. He conquered much of the Asian continent during his time in power, starting with Transoxiana. His empire eventually extended from the Mediterranean Sea to the Himalayas and from the Caucasus to the Arabian Sea. In many instances he did more than defeat. He decimated. Some estimates put his death toll at nineteen million. That's a lot of skull towers.

But he was also a patron of the arts and sciences. He filled Samarkand, the capital of his empire, with scholars and artists and physicians and scientists from all the lands he conquered. He also commissioned amazing feats of architecture, such as Registan Square. He didn't spend too much time in his capital among his beautiful buildings, though. He preferred the tent city of his army and was too busy conquering other places to dally long in palaces.

His fame spread into Europe, where he was called Tamerlane, which means Timur the Lame, due to injuries to his right hand and leg that he sustained during his days as a soldier.

In the winter of 1405 he was on his way to add China to his empire when he died en route in Kazakhstan, at the age of sixty-eight. His body was brought to Samarkand and interred. The Timurid empire would last for less than a hundred years after Timur's death, but the man's notoriety as a vicious vanquisher was permanent-markered in the history books.

Except in Uzbekistan. They love him in Uzbekistan. His homeland erected multiple statues of the conqueror, some of them in god-sized dimensions, positioning him as a cultural unifier in a multifarious culture that had to remake itself after the dissolution of the USSR.

They also still have his body. Timur's tomb in Samarkand is called Gur-e-Amir – Tomb of the King. The most prominent feature of the mausoleum is its large, ribbed, sky-blue dome. On either side of that dome are massive freestanding pillars jutting into the sky like tusks. The terra-cotta building is covered in blue and white tiles arranged in intricate patterns and mosaics. It's both simple and extravagant.

The first clue that Timur left behind a curse was revealed three and a half centuries later. In 1740 a warlord named Nadir Shah stole the slab of black jade that Timur had been buried under and took it back to his home in Persia. Somehow the slab broke in two, and it is said that Nadir Shah suffered bad luck from that point on, until he was convinced to return the slab to Samarkand.

Almost two hundred years later, in 1924, Uzbekistan became part of the domain of the USSR. Then, on June 19, 1941, the curse story got more interesting. Soviet archeologists became curious about the conqueror's tomb, so they exhumed Timur's body under orders from Joseph Stalin, despite protests by the citizens of Samarkand.

The team was led by anthropologist Mikhail Gerasimov. They discovered was a body that was 5 feet 6 inches tall, with wounds in its right hip and two fingers missing from the right hand, validating Timur's nickname, Tamerlane. Later they would ship his remains to Moscow to reconstruct his facial features based on his skull, a technique that Gerasimov pioneered.

Days later, Hitler and Germany invaded the Soviet Union. Immediately the two events were linked together. How could they not be? The exhuming of one bloody dictator was quickly followed by the appearance of another. The two events became so intertwined that rumors began to swirl about inscriptions on the tomb and casket. The one on the tomb is supposed to read, "When I rise from the dead, the world shall tremble." When the Soviet archeologists ignored that warning, they allegedly found another curse etched into Timur's casket: "Whosoever opens my tomb shall unleash an invader more terrible than I." Adolph Hitler is pretty terrible.

Unfortunately, no evidence of either inscription exists. However, two years later, after the analysis was complete and the archeologists reinterred Timur's remains, Soviet forces defeated the Nazis at Stalingrad. It was a major turning point in World War II.

Why Timur's tomb would be cursed in the first place is unknown. Maybe it was wishful thinking on the part of the people of Samarkand who didn't want either eighteenth-century or twentieth-century warlords disturbing the bones of their hero.

Or maybe it was because Timur was never meant to be interred in that mausoleum. He was supposed to be laid to rest in a custom-built tomb fit for an emperor in Shahrisabz, the city where he was born. Instead, he ended up in Samarkand in a tomb built for his grandson, Muhammed Sultan. When Timur died on the way to China, the roads to Shahrisabz were impassible due to the same snowy conditions that had killed him. So he was buried in the easier-to-reach city of Samarkand instead. And maybe he's grumpy about that.

There's something fitting about a warlord so bloodthirsty that not even death could stop his murderous rampage.

The Black Angel

CURRENT LOCATION: OAKLAND CEMETERY, IOWA CITY, IOWA	**CREATED FOR:** TERESA FELDEVERT AND FAMILY
MATERIAL: BRONZE	**YEAR OF INSTALLATION:** 1912–1913
SCULPTOR: MARIO KORBEL	

It was once an eight-foot-tall shimmering bronze memorial to a young son and a dear husband. Today it is a blackened horror of a figure with a deathly curse. You can say hi to it during the cemetery's open hours.

Oakland Cemetery in Iowa City, Iowa, was established in 1843. It covers about forty acres, is Protestant, and is full of the usual plain, rectangular tombstones and dead people. Nothing too out of the ordinary and nothing much worth mentioning, as far as cemeteries go. Except for the giant black angel dominating the landscape and terrifying visitors.

Angel statues in cemeteries are extremely common. There are millions of them spreading their stone wings across the dead in America and Europe. So many, in fact, that the wondrous image of a person with feathery wings has become as bland a sight as a rectangular tombstone in a cemetery.

But not the Black Angel. The Black Angel has transcended blandness by going full-on spooky. And being full-on spooky in a cemetery has earned it an abundance of creepy legends. It also, strangely enough, makes the statue better at memorializing the dead beneath its feet. People will forget a boring funerary statue, but they'll talk for generations about a scary one.

The statue is eight and a half feet tall and stands atop a square pedestal that lifts it to a full thirteen feet. It depicts a winged woman in a flowing dress, her head tilted down so that her face is usually in shadow. Her massive wings are at odd, asymmetrical angles – one extended out perpendicular to her body and the other drooping like it's broken. Her arms are aligned with her wings, giving the strange impression that she's wearing fake wings strapped to her arms. There's something rounded and clay-like about her features. She looks like she belongs in a fantasy cemetery in a Tim Burton movie instead of in a real-death cemetery in Iowa.

The bronze artwork was crafted by Mario Korbel, a Czech sculptor based in Chicago. When it was placed in the cemetery in the early 1910s, it shone golden and glorious. *Rodina Feldevertova* is inscribed on the front of the stone pedestal, which means "The Feldevert Family" in Czech. It is accompanied by a tall stone carved into the shape of a tree trunk.

This Iowa plot is the lasting work of Teresa Feldevert, a Czech midwife. The stone tree came first, and was planted to memorialize her son from her first marriage, Edward Dolezal. He died at age eighteen after contracting meningitis. It was the second son she lost; the first, Otto, died two weeks before she moved to the United States.

Childless and husbandless, Teresa left Iowa City and lived in a few different places before ending up in Eugene,

Oregon, where she met Nicholas Feldevert, whom she eventually married. He preceded her in death and left her somewhat wealthy. One of the first things she did with that money was commission the angel sculpture. She ended up fighting with Korbel because she wanted the tree trunk gravestone to be incorporated into the sculpture of the angel, but in the end they were kept separate. Regardless, the angel became the repository of the remains of both her son Edward and her husband. Finally, in 1924, Teresa herself was laid to rest beneath the angel she had commissioned, although the memorial bears only her birth date. It's a beautiful story, each family member succumbing to the inevitable and then being reunited beneath a shining statue for all to see.

But then the angel aged, and the red-gold bronze oxidized to deep black, as if dark forces had tainted it. Corrupted it. Cursed it. Normally, we call those forces time and weather. But in this case, because of the stature of the statue and the strange angle of its wings, and the fact that it doesn't fit in with the rest of the cemetery (*and* because it's in a cemetery in the first place), the change in color seems malevolent.

Some say it was the addition of Teresa's ashes that cursed the statue, that she had cheated on her husband and that the glowing angel looming above the ostensibly loving family could no longer take part in the ruse. However, the angel started turning black within ten years of being installed – while Teresa was still alive.

The Black Angel has accrued as many stories as there are paranormal books and websites. The most common story is that if you touch the statue, you'll die. And for whatever reason, "touching" is often specifically called out as kissing. Also, if a pregnant woman crosses through the shadow of the Black Angel, the woman will miscarry. (It's a common enough legend that pregnant women in general might want to avoid rot-yards.) A man is said to have gone mad after breaking off the statue's thumbs. And, in fact, she is missing a few digits. Another myth is that if a virgin is kissed in front of the statue, it will restore the Black Angel to her previous glowing form, although we can probably guess why that legend started. It's also said that every Halloween, the statue grows blacker.

It's a popular spook spot for thrill seekers and paranormal investigators, a rite of passage for students, and, according to some locals, an icon of the city. What it is more than anything can be found in the last two lines of the epitaph on the stone tree trunk beside the Black Angel:

> Do not weep for me, dear mother.
> I am at peace in my cool grave.

The Black Angel is definitely a cool grave.

How to Curse an Object

Most of this book is a lesson in defense: how to avoid cursed objects (e.g., don't exhume bodies, stop buying expensive gems, and stay away from old dolls). But what if you want to take the offensive? What if you want to curse an object? How would you go about doing that?

Turns out, there are a ton of ways. Every culture and religion and group on the planet seems to have their own method of cursing objects. It's apparently a very human thing to do.

Ancient Greeks and Romans inscribed flat pieces of lead and stone with curses. Thousands of these curse tablets have been dug up all over Europe. Early Christians in Ireland and Scotland had *bullaun*, or cursing stones, which had depressions in them. To use, the curser would place a smaller stone in the depression and turn it over while wishing misfortune on another. Vikings carved curses into poles called nithing poles, stuck horse heads atop them, and planted them in the ground facing the intended victim's home. In Japan, curses can be cast using wooden plaques called *ema*, which are inscribed with ill wishes and hung at special sites called *enkiri* (tie-cutting shrines). In India, lemons and chilies are used both as protection and as a curse. Stringing them together and hanging them up in a display that's called *nimbu mirchi* can ward off evil, but throwing one of these objects on a busy roadway can cause evil to befall a passerby. And people on every continent — from Africa to Europe to Asia to America — curse effigies and dolls.

Some say you can curse any object by merely holding it and thinking negative thoughts directed at an individual. Which tells me that, in the end, the objects and methods don't really matter. It's the thought that counts.

The Gravestone of Carl Pruitt

PLACE OF ORIGIN:	CURRENT LOCATION:
PULASKI COUNTY, KENTUCKY	UNKNOWN
YEAR OF INSTALLATION:	DEATH TOLL:
1938	FIVE

The southeastern edge of Pulaski County, Kentucky, is leprous with strip mines. These swaths of denuded earth can be landscape eyesores, environmentally dodgy, much needed sources of jobs, and rich pockets of economically important resources, depending on where you fall in the argument. But one of these myriad strip mines is a little different from the others. It generates a different kind of argument. It may, or may not, have saved humanity from a cursed object.

A lot of cursed objects are supposed to be deadly, but the gravestone of Carl Pruitt is absolutely bloodthirsty. According to the lore, it has caused the deaths of five different people, each of them strangled by chains.

The story goes like this: The year is 1938. Carl Pruitt returns home, his fingers full of splinters and his lungs full of sawdust from his job as a carpenter. He's early, and he's looking forward to seeing his wife. Which he does – naked and in bed with another man. Pruitt flies into a rage and attacks his wife, while the naked man takes an awkward post-coital flight out the nearest window.

Pruitt grabs a nearby length of chain and wraps it around his wife's throat, strangling her until she's dead. Immediately, the grief and the shame and the irrevocability of the act sink in, so he grabs a gun and shoots himself in the face. It's a terrible, although not outlandish, story. But what happens next takes it over the top.

Pruitt's body was buried in a nearby cemetery. Legend says that over time, a section of the headstone that marked his grave discolored, developing a chain-shaped stain across its face. Locals became fixated on the story of the murder-suicide and the stained stone. And it's the headstone that distinguishes this story from your average graveyard haunting.

Sometime after the gravestone was planted, a group of boys biked to the site. One boy, James Collins, pelted it with rocks. The projectiles chipped and cracked the block of granite. When they got bored, the gang took off toward home. But James Collins immediately lost control of his bicycle and hit a tree. When the boys checked to see if he was okay, they found him dead – but not from a head wound. In the collision, his bike chain had somehow wrapped itself around his neck and strangled him. The next day, the pockmarks from Collins's stone projectiles were gone. The gravestone was marred only by the chain stain.

Weeks later, Collins's mother flew into a rage of grief and took off to the cemetery with a pickax in her hands. She demolished Pruitt's stone and then went home to do the laundry. As she was hanging sheets on the line to dry – a line that for some reason was actually a chain – it wrapped itself around her neck and strangled her. When locals went to see the damage that had been her doing (and undoing), they found Carl Pruitt's gravestone in one piece and as shiny as new (plus a chain-shaped stain).

The story of the supernatural stone spread, and eventually someone else decided to test the curse. A farmer driving by the cemetery in a horse-drawn cart shot at the headstone with a gun. His horses took off running, pitching the farmer forward and over the front of the cart, where he died with the trace chain of the harness wrapped around his throat. Carl Pruitt's gravestone was undamaged.

At one point a pair of police officers went to investigate what was becoming a big story in those parts. One of the men made fun of the stone and the story. Upon leaving the cemetery, they were chased by a light that panicked the doubting officer, who was driving the squad car. He swerved between two posts and crashed. The officer in the passenger seat was thrown clear and lived. The driver was found dead, strangled by a chain that connected the two posts.

The final death bandied about around campfires in southeastern Kentucky involved a man who became so fed up with the cursed object that he took a hammer and chisel to it. His blows rang out through the night until they ended with a loud scream. Locals found him dead, with the chain from the graveyard gate wrapped around his neck. The hammer and chisel were both there, but no chisel marks could be found on Carl Pruitt's grave.

That was one chain-strangling too many. Locals started selling their cemetery plots and exhuming their loved ones to move their bodies out of the graveyard and away from its cursed stone. Eventually, the cemetery was reduced to a single plot, topped by one chain-stained gravestone. And that gravestone might have kept on killing had the land not been sold to a mining company and the entire area turned into a strip mine in 1958. It's assumed that the stone ended up with the rest of the rubble from the mine, buried and waiting for some future archeologist to find it and unchain the curse all over again.

A single black-and-white photo is always tied to this story. It shows a man in overalls and a large newsboy hat leaning against the back of an old car. Nobody knows whether it's a photo of Carl Pruitt or how exactly it became attached to the story. The earliest source of the tale seems to be the late Michael Paul Henson's *More Kentucky Ghost Stories*, which was published in 1996.

Researchers have tried to locate Pruitt's death certificate without success, but they have found a death record in Louisville, Kentucky, from 1950, for an Enos C. Prewitt . . . who died of a self-inflicted gunshot wound.

All that aside, we're left with a solid moral: don't disrespect the gravestones of angry killers.

The Bronze Lady

CURRENT LOCATION:	CREATED FOR:
SLEEPY HOLLOW CEMETERY, SLEEPY HOLLOW, NEW YORK	GENERAL SAMUEL RUSSELL THOMAS
SCULPTOR:	**YEAR OF INSTALLATION:**
ANDREW O'CONNOR JR.	1903
MODEL:	**ALSO KNOWN AS:**
JESS PHOEBE BROWN	*RECUEILLEMENT*

The Old Dutch Church Burying Ground and its neighbor Sleepy Hollow Cemetery in Sleepy Hollow, New York, are famous for their connections to Washington Irving and his 1820 story *The Legend of Sleepy Hollow*. But there is another dark force besides the Headless Horseman at work amongst those graves. She is called the Bronze Lady.

Washington Irving buried his fictional horseman in the Old Dutch Church Burying Ground, and in the story, it is from there that the dark rider gallops forth to claim the heads of nervous schoolteachers. The Old Dutch Church itself rises above the gravestones on the far side of the bridge that is the finish line for anyone being chased by the headless fiend. Meanwhile, Sleepy Hollow Cemetery, which is newer and shares a border with the older cemetery, became the final resting place of Washington Irving following his death in 1859.

The Old Dutch Burying Ground occupies 2.5 acres directly behind the church. It was founded around 1685. Sleepy Hollow Cemetery is much larger, about 90 acres, and opened in 1849. Besides Washington Irving, members of such wealthy New York families as the Rockefellers, Carnegies, Chryslers, and Astors also molder here. Irving was instrumental in the newer cemetery's development, as well as its name. The village where it's located was then known as North Tarrytown, and the town's leaders originally proposed to name the burial ground Tarrytown Cemetery. Irving successfully pressured them to dismiss their first choice for his preferred Sleepy Hollow Cemetery. A century and a half later, in 1997, the name of the village was also changed to Sleepy Hollow, to capitalize on the famous spooky story set there.

But there's another spooky story set there. The Bronze Lady of Sleepy Hollow Cemetery has had to live in the shadow of the Headless Horseman even though she . . . is real.

The Bronze Lady is a larger-than-life statue of a woman seated with her eyes closed and her two hands clasping one of her knees. A shroud covers her hair and a flowing robe covers her body. Unlike most other graveyard statues, time and the elements haven't conspired to make her especially creepy. She looks exactly like what she is — a large, dark statue of a woman.

She's squeezed between two pine trees and faces a large, square mausoleum, which houses the tomb of General Samuel Russell Thomas. Thomas earned his stars in the Civil War, ascending the ranks of the Union from second lieutenant to brigadier general. After the war, he ascended the tax bracket with the same gusto, making it big in the pig iron, coal, and railroad industries — big enough for his corpse to be marked with both a large mausoleum and a statue.

Even though the statue and mausoleum are part of the same memorial, the way they are situated is unusual, and that arrangement may be the inspiration for the curse. The female form faces the mausoleum as if she's not there to be looked at, but to look. Almost like she's guarding it. Or waiting for someone to walk through the green bronze doors. The effect is unintentionally eerie. So eerie, in fact, that many locals have grown up swapping stories about how the statue is cursed.

Tales are told of crying sounds coming from the Bronze Lady. Some claim to have felt actual tears on her cheeks. Kids sneak out there at Halloween and dare each other to touch the statue. If you peek through the keyhole of the mausoleum or knock on its metal doors, it's said that you'll have nightmares. If you treat the statue with violence – say, kick her shins or slap her face or spit on her – she will haunt you for the rest of your life. In one story, if you peek through the keyhole *after* abusing the statue, you'll see a red eye staring back at you. Another claims that to break the curse, you need to slap the statue again and then knock three times on the mausoleum door.

Strangely, there is a positive legend of the statue as well: if you are nice to her, she will protect you for the rest of your life. And evidently, many people hold to this superstition; cemetery staff often find coins in her lap.

The sculpture was created by Andrew O'Connor Jr. at the behest of the general's widow, Ann Augusta Porter Thomas, after her husband's death on January 14, 1903. The statue's name is *Recueillement* (French for "contemplation"). The model for the sculpture was Jess Phoebe Brown, one of O'Connor's favorite models.

According to the 1995 book *The Sculptors O'Connor* by Doris Flodin Soderman, when Mrs. Thomas visited O'Connor's studio to check on the statue that she had commissioned, she didn't like the way it looked. She wanted the statue to appear happier – maybe more hopeful about the family's post-death prospects. O'Connor dutifully asked his client to give him another week to address her feedback. When Mrs. Thomas returned, he showed her a new cast of the head bearing a much happier expression. Mrs. Thomas declared it perfect, at which point O'Connor dashed the head to the floor, smashing it into pieces, and said, "I just made this to show you that I could do it, but I should never let such a monstrosity out of my studio."

Inside the mausoleum, only two crypts are marked with

names: Samuel Russell Thomas and his son Edward. Mrs. Thomas wasn't interred there. As for Edward, even though his name appears on a crypt, the cemetery has no record of anybody being interred there.

Maybe if O'Connor had listened to Mrs. Thomas, his work of art wouldn't be cursed today. But then again, maybe that was inevitable. In *The Legend of Sleepy Hollow*, Washington Irving characterized the people of the valley this way:

> They are given to all kinds of marvellous beliefs, are subject to trances and visions, and frequently see strange sights, and hear music and voices in the air. The whole neighborhood abounds with local tales, haunted spots, and twilight superstitions. . . .

Maybe any bronze funerary figure would have transmogrified into a cursed object in the home of the Headless Horseman.

Shakespeare's Grave

CURRENT LOCATION:
HOLY TRINITY CHURCH, STRATFORD-UPON-AVON, ENGLAND

SIGNIFICANCE:
BURIAL SITE OF THE BARD OF AVON

AGE:
~400 YEARS

William Shakespeare knew how to sling a curse. Some form of that word appears 197 times in his forty or so plays, if I'm using Open Source Shakespeare correctly. But we don't need to scour the collected dramatic works of the man whose pen evolved the English language beyond grunts and sniffs to know how good the playwright was with a curse. We just have to go check out his grave.

William Shakespeare was born in 1564 in the English town of Stratford-upon-Avon, northwest of London, to a glove-maker father and a farmer mother. He married Anne Hathaway at the age of eighteen and had three children with her. He moved to London and found success as an actor, playwright, and partner in a theater company. When he was forty-nine, he returned to his hometown, where he died three years later. Meanwhile, he completely transformed the English language and fully stocked our common pool of metaphors.

Besides a handful of biographical facts and his life's work of plays and poetry, little is known about Shakespeare. Even the circumstances and cause of his death in 1616 are lost to history. But we do know that his grave is cursed. It says so right there on the stone slab.

But before we get to his grave, let's talk about another curse Shakespeare is known for – *Macbeth*. His play about a Scottish general's murderous rise to the Scottish throne is one of his most popular. However, actors who perform it balk at saying the title of the play inside a theater for fear of bringing bad luck to themselves and the production. As a result, they often refer to *Macbeth* as "the Scottish play" or "the Bard's play." The exception to the curse is if the actor says the word while rehearsing for or performing the play.

The story goes that a coven of witches was angered that Shakespeare included witches and incantations in the play and so they placed a curse on it. According to the Royal Shakespeare Company website, if the name of the Play-That-Must-Not-Be-Named does slip through an actor's lips, the way to defeat the curse is to leave the theater, spin around thrice, spit, curse, and then knock on the door of the theater to regain entrance.

But that's just a curse for actors to worry about. Shakespeare's other curse could impact anyone who visits his grave. Because even though he's been called the Immortal Bard, Shakespeare went to dirt like the rest of us. And that dirt can be found under a church in Stratford-upon-Avon.

Holy Trinity Church is both the site of Shakespeare's baptism as a child and his burial at the end of his life. Historians also like to assign both his birthday and death day as April 23, giving a nice symmetry to his life. The church building dates to the thirteenth century. It's located on the banks of the River Avon on an atmospheric piece of land punctured by ancient gravestones. But Shakespeare isn't buried in the graveyard. He's inside the church, interred with his wife and eldest daughter, Susanna, in the floor of the chancel (where the altar is located). A nearby monument depicts the Bard from the waist up with quill and parchment in hand and is topped by a pair of cherubs and a ghastly skull. The grave is a simple slab of stone in the floor. His name isn't even engraved on it. Where another stone might feature the familiar "Here lies" refrain are the lines of a curse that can barely be made out in the old rock, but which are transcribed on a helpful plaque atop the grave:

> **Good friend for Jesus sake forbear,**
> **To dig the dust enclosed here.**
> **Blessed be the man that spares these stones,**
> **And cursed be he that moves my bones.**

The story goes that Shakespeare himself composed this funerary verse, and for reasons that weren't poetic, but practical. At the time of his death, bodies were often exhumed for medical research, to make room for newly dead bodies, or even so their treasures could be grave-robbed. In Shakespeare's case, there was also the risk of fans wanting to take souvenirs. Writing the verse was Shakespeare's way of guaranteeing he could spend eternity with a "Do Not Disturb" sign dangling from his door handle.

And the people of England take the curse seriously. In 2008, the burial site and other stone surfaces in the church needed to be restored, having begun to crumble with age and use. The team overseeing the project had to assure the people of England that they wouldn't disturb the bones of Shakespeare and that they were taking all precautions to minimize disruption to the grave.

But, the thing is, Shakespeare's bones might have already been disturbed centuries ago. It has long been rumored that his skull is no longer rotting with the rest of him – that at some point it went missing from the grave. Of course, this seems like an obvious rumor to spread about the author of that indelible scene in *Hamlet* in which the Danish prince talks to the skull of his friend, "poor Yorick."

In 2016, a team of researchers used ground-penetrating radar — the type that wouldn't disturb Shakespeare's bones or activate the curse — to see if they could find either evidence of the skull or the lack thereof. What they found were possible signs of a past disturbance of the area of the grave where the skull would be. Interesting, but inconclusive.

So until somebody ignores the curse completely and roots around Shakespeare's remains for definitive answers, the question of his skull will remain a mystery. Unless, that is, there's another option.

A professor named Francis Thackeray, from the University of Witwatersrand in Johannesburg, has an idea. In a 2015 interview with the *Telegraph*, he posited a way to reach Shakespeare's skull while avoiding the curse. He said: "We could possibly get around that by at least exposing the bones and doing high-resolution non-destructive laser surface scanning for forensic analyses, without moving a single bone. Besides, Shakespeare said nothing about teeth in that epitaph."

Hopefully, Shakespeare's curse is forgiving when it comes to technicalities.

This Book Is Cursed!

You are holding in your hands, right now, a cursed object. That's thanks to the curse printed on page 11, the one that prescribes the penalty for its theft as hanging and eye gouging by ravens.

It might seem like an aggressive tone to set for the book, but this curse furthers an ancient tradition that can be traced back at least as far as the seventh century BCE, when King Assurbanipal of Assyria had clay tablets in his collection inscribed with threats of divine retribution against anybody who stole or inscribed their own name on them.

Book cursing really took off in medieval Europe when scribes would endure backbreaking, eye-dimming, hand-cramping work to meticulously create a single book. And they wanted to protect those books. Not just because they represented so much painstaking labor, but because stealing a book often meant stealing a one-of-a-kind set of human knowledge in the days before mass production. Book curses were like an ancient form of copyright protection. Except when you broke that copyright, instead of jail time and fines, ravens would peck your eyes out. Or worse.

The practice of book cursing continued to at least the nineteenth century, long past the era when a book was a cheap commodity not exactly worth a person's body or soul. The curse at the beginning of this book originated in Germany in the 1800s, written by an unknown scribe who might have been more interested in playing around with language than in supernaturally protecting his work. Each line of the curse began in Latin and ended in German.

Serious effects of other book curses throughout the centuries include roasting in a frying pan, contracting fatal illness, drowning, being torn apart by pigs, and suffering death and damnation. Capital punishments all. So, hopefully, you didn't steal this book.

Cursed in the Attic

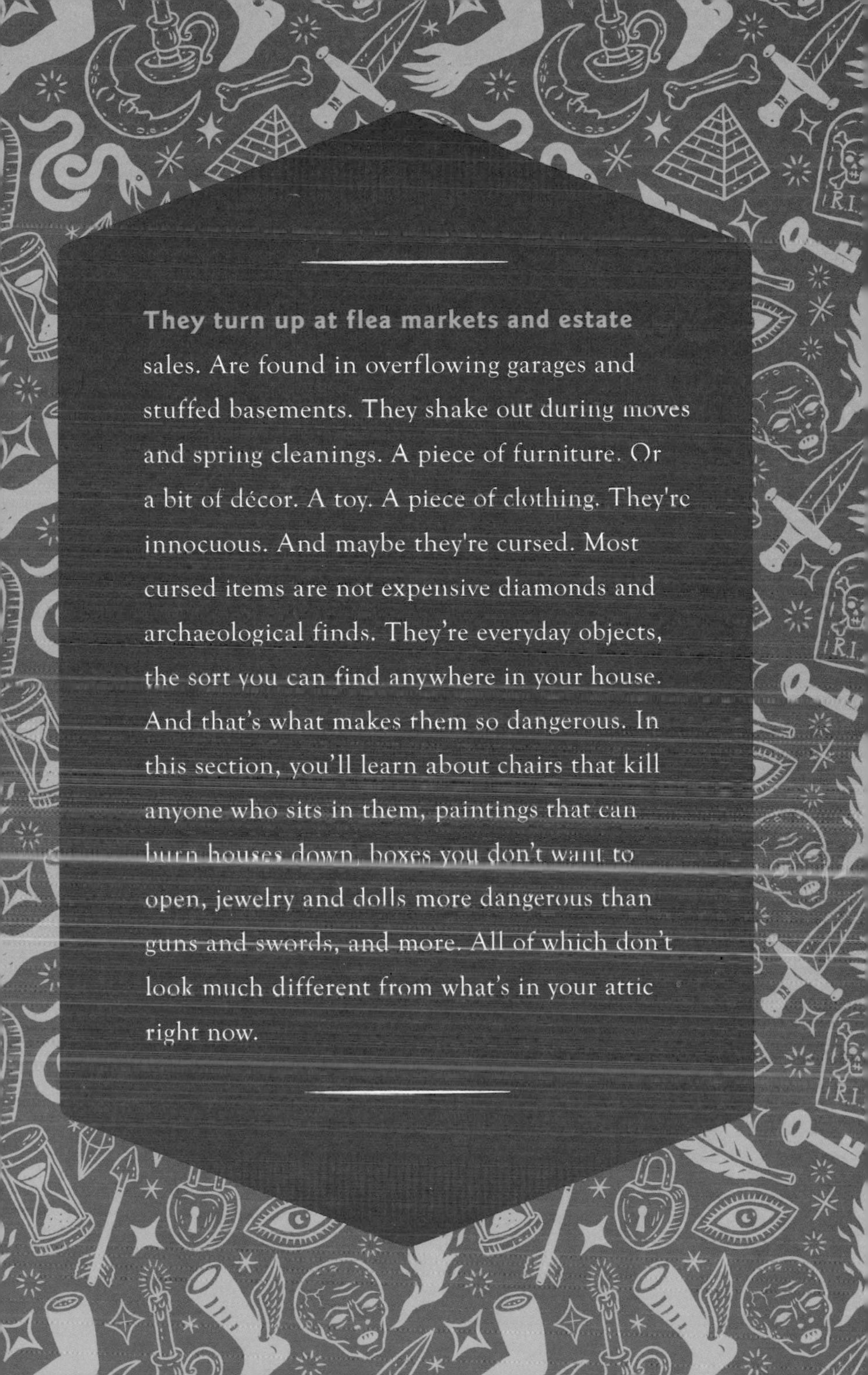

They turn up at flea markets and estate sales. Are found in overflowing garages and stuffed basements. They shake out during moves and spring cleanings. A piece of furniture. Or a bit of décor. A toy. A piece of clothing. They're innocuous. And maybe they're cursed. Most cursed items are not expensive diamonds and archaeological finds. They're everyday objects, the sort you can find anywhere in your house. And that's what makes them so dangerous. In this section, you'll learn about chairs that kill anyone who sits in them, paintings that can burn houses down, boxes you don't want to open, jewelry and dolls more dangerous than guns and swords, and more. All of which don't look much different from what's in your attic right now.

The Crying Boy Paintings

CURRENT LOCATION:	DECADES OF ORIGIN:
VARIOUS	1950S–1970S
PAINTED BY:	PAINTER PSEUDONYMS:
BRUNO AMADIO AND ANNA ZINKEISEN	GIOVANNI BRAGOLIN, FRANCHOT SEVILLE

There's bad art, and then there's bad art. The former doesn't conform to conventional ideas of aesthetics, creativity, and skill. The latter burns down the house of anyone who hangs it above their mantel. A good example of this second type is an infamous series of European paintings, all called *The Crying Boy*.

This particular cursed object story is of relatively recent vintage. It comes from the 1980s, the same decade that told us Smurf merchandise was full of demons and rock bands were brainwashing listeners by hiding Satanic messages on their albums. It was a fascinating decade of modern mythmaking.

On September 4, 1985, the British tabloid *The Sun* published an article entitled "Blazing Curse of the Crying Boy." The story was republished from a regional rag from

Rotherham, which had run the story two days earlier. It was the perfect eye-yanker of a headline. But the article that followed delivered on its promise.

The story centered on a tragedy suffered by the Hall family. A large section of their house had been gutted by flames, except for one item: a cheap department-store painting of a teary boy. Now, that in itself wasn't the kindling for the legend. After all, fire is fickle – in a house turned ash, something inevitably survives. What fanned the flames was a quote from a fireman at the scene. He asserted that the artwork was one of many such mass-produced crying child paintings that always seemed to survive fires and that the fire department had amassed some fifty examples of them since the early 1970s.

Three astounding ideas can be extrapolated from the fireman's assertion. One: that these generic paintings had been surviving fires for more than a decade. Two: that houses with these paintings seemed prone to fire. And three: that the incendiary powers of the portrait didn't lie solely with the original

but could be transferred through copies. In a world overrun with mass-marketed goods, this is probably the most horrifying idea of the three. But the takeaway, at least according to *The Sun*, was clear: every print of *The Crying Boy* was cursed.

The idea terrified a sizeable number of owners of the reproductions. After *The Sun* invited readers to send in their prints, it received 2,500 renderings of sad children from across England. Interestingly, they weren't all of the same boy. Some included multiple crying children. And sometimes the subject was a girl. But all of the paintings depicted children who, apparently, cried tears that could extinguish fires.

The Sun burned all the portraits in a pyre on Halloween. Afterward, the paper published a photo of the blaze attended by a blonde woman in a fire hat and jean shorts, one of its controversial Page Three girls.

The legend grew from then, cultivated over years by both media coverage and public interest. A backstory for the subject of the original painting was fleshed out. Reportedly, the boy's name was Don Bonillo, and he accidentally killed his parents in a fire in their home in Spain. Fire followed the boy wherever he went, giving him the nickname Diablo. Orphaned, the boy was kept and abused by a priest, and then also abused by the artist who painted his weepy portrait. His short life ended in a car explosion in the 1970s. An iconic crying child can only have a sad life, after all. The child was never identified. And, as was already mentioned, there's no single child subject; multiple versions of these paintings feature different crying children.

As for the painter, the name Giovanni Bragolin is a common signature on the crying child paintings. But Bragolin doesn't exist. At one point in the chain of lore it was hypothesized that Bragolin was a pseudonym for another painter named Franchot Seville. But Franchot Seville doesn't exist, either. Both Seville and Bragolin were found to be pseudonyms for a Russian doll of a Spanish painter named Bruno Amadio, who *did* exist.

Amadio painted lots of crying children portraits, copies of which were sold in department stores all over England throughout the '50s, '60s, and '70s. Complicating matters further, another artist, Anna Zinkeisen of Scotland, was creating portraits of depressed adolescents and offering prints through the same channels. Both were deceased by the time the curse rumors began to bubble up.

Many of the extremely specific story details, especially surrounding the subjects of some of the paintings, were published by *The Sun* and another British tabloid, the *Daily Mirror*, both of which aimed to capitalize on this incendiary story to the fullest extent.

A quarter of a century later, the story was still going strong in the United Kingdom. In 2010 Steve Punt, a comedian with a BBC show, decided to test the legend on television. He got his hands on a copy of *The Crying Child* and burned it on camera. (You can see the footage on YouTube.) Remarkably, the painting didn't burn. The fire merely scorched one corner.

After subsequent testing, Punt concluded that the painting had some kind of fire-retardant finish on it. He also noted that in a burning house, the string it hung from would probably snap first, dropping the portrait on its face. That, combined with the fireproof varnish, is likely what protected the images.

It's an interesting hypothesis – one that anybody can test, actually, because you can still buy copies of *The Crying Child* today. Although you probably shouldn't.

The Baleroy Chair of Death

PLACE OF ORIGIN:	LAST KNOWN LOCATION:
FRANCE	BALEROY MANSION, PHILADELPHIA, PENNSYLVANIA
AGE: 200 YEARS	DEATH TOLL: THREE
NOTABLE OWNERS: GEORGE MEADE EASBY, NAPOLEON BONAPARTE	

Chairs are among the most mundane items on the planet. They were invented because our legs get tired and we don't like our butts getting dirty on the floor. Yet, under the right conditions, chairs can be terrifying. And the best condition is, of course, cursed.

The Baleroy Chair of Death is a good example of a bad chair. This stately cursed object is a 200-year-old blue upholstered wing chair. If you've ever toured an old mansion, you've probably seen a piece of furniture like it. And, in fact, its last known location was in its namesake, the Baleroy Mansion in Philadelphia, Pennsylvania. But those are the boring facts about it. Its legends are far more interesting, if somewhat lacking in detail.

The lore goes that a warlock made the chair sometime in the nineteenth century, although his name and reason for making the chair (other than needing a place to sit) have been lost to time. The chair is also supposed to have been owned (and presumably sat on) by Napoleon Bonaparte. Since the chair was installed at Baleroy Mansion, it's been said that a ghost named either Amelia or Amanda manifests herself as a red mist to lure people to sit in it. However, the thing that gives this object a place at the cursed table is that its owner accused it of ending the lives of at least three people.

Baleroy Mansion looms over Mermaid Lane in the wealthy Chestnut Hill area of Philadelphia. The thirty-two-room stone structure dates to 1911 and, at least from the outside, looks sort of bland for a mansion, like a rather engorged but otherwise everyday suburban house. Inside, though, is a different story.

In 1926, Major May Stevenson Easby, his wife Henrietta, and his two young sons George and Steven moved into the house that they would dub Baleroy. They spent much of their time there stuffing it full of antiques . . . and ghost stories.

We can thank the elder son, George Meade Easby, for these tales. He was eight years old when his family moved into the mansion and remained a resident for three-quarters of a century, until his death in 2005 at the age of eighty-seven. He loved ghost stories, and his unceasing contributions to the Baleroy lore, as well as his passionate advertisement of it, prompted some to anoint the mansion "the most haunted house in Philadelphia" and others "the most haunted home in America."

Easby claimed to have seen the ghost of the original owner of the mansion, a carpenter who murdered his wife inside the house. One day shortly after they moved in, while Easby and his brother Steven were playing in the fountain in the yard, Easby claimed that Steven's reflection transformed into a skull. He died not long after, at age eleven, of an unknown disease. There were the ghostly arms that would grab Easby in his sleep. An ectoplasm sometimes floated down the hall. The kitchen cabinets opened and closed by themselves. Phantom cars would drive up to the house and disappear. The ghost of Thomas Jefferson haunted the dining room, and a woman

dressed in black would sometimes appear in the house, as would a monk wearing a beige robe.

Easby once told a reporter for *People* magazine, "I enjoy living here, but it's quite an adventure." He embraced most of the ghosts in the house. He even believed that his brother and mother hung around in spirit after their deaths and that the latter had led him to secret family treasures stashed in the house. The article, which appeared in the October 1994 issue, includes a black-and-white portrait of Easby. He's sitting in a chair (assumedly uncursed), his white hair standing on end, his mouth open in creepy glee, and a wispy presence hovering behind him. In his hand is a small portrait of his mother. It looks like a promotional still from a horror movie, and indeed Easby tried to act in and produce low-budget films for a while. In short, he seems exactly the type of person who would keep a cursed chair around for kicks.

The antiques and ghosts surrounding Easby gave his imagination ample fodder for his movies, especially the Napoleonic pieces that were a major part of the collection. His family had an interest in French artifacts, and Baleroy itself was named after a place in France. But the one object that has risen above all the other ghastly tales of the mansion is the Chair of Death.

It was believed to have been kept in the house's Blue Room, which was styled as an eighteenth-century drawing room. It's said that Easby strung a rope across the seat and forbade the posteriors of guests after enough people perished as a result of sitting in it. Easby told the authors of the 1989 book *Haunted Houses U.S.A.* that one of his housekeepers sat in the chair, collapsed, and died a few hours later. The next victim was a cousin of Easby's, and the third a friend named

Paul Kimmens. Both died within weeks, and, according to Easby, none of them believed in the curse. Whether any of them saw the red mist of Amanda/Amelia is unknown.

Easby never married nor had children, so after he died, the mansion opened to the public for a while, despite the dangers of the Chair of Death. A lucky few visitors got to tour the infamous home while the valuable antiques were on view. Some have since been donated to museums. Others were sold, and eventually, so was the house. Today it's a private residence. And the residents might have one more ghost on their hands. Before his death, Easby was quoted in a 1984 article in the *Chestnut Hill Local* as saying, "When I leave here, I'm coming back to haunt them — if they don't take good care of this place I'm going to be right back there after them."

Whether the Chair of Death survived the estate transfer after Easby joined Amanda/Amelia, his mother, and the rest of the spirits in the house, nobody knows. But if you're feeling brave, you can go up to the porch, ring the doorbell, and find out easily enough.

Although the last thing you might hear is, "Have a seat, and we'll be right with you."

The Dybbuk Box

PLACE OF ORIGIN:
SPAIN OR NEW YORK

CONTENTS:
TWO 1920S WHEAT PENNIES, TWO LOCKS OF HAIR, A GRANITE STATUE, A DRIED ROSEBUD, A WINE CUP, A CANDLE HOLDER, AND A DYBBUK

CURRENT LOCATION:
ZAK BAGANS'S THE HAUNTED MUSEUM, LAS VEGAS, NEVADA

PREVIOUS OWNERS:
KEVIN MANNIS, IOSIF NIETZKE, JASON HAXTON

In Jewish folklore, a dybbuk is an evil spirit, sometimes defined as the soul of a dead person that has become perverted in its afterlife. Its name means "to cling," and that's what it does, Saran Wrapping itself to the soul of a living person to very bad ends. But when you stuff one into a box, that box becomes a cursed object. And the most infamous dybbuk box story — the first dybbuk box story, in fact — is borne not of ancient folklore, but of twenty-first-century digital platforms and pop culture celebrities.

In 2001, a man named Kevin Mannis visited an estate sale in Portland, Oregon, to see if there were any nice pieces he could pick up for his used furniture business. The house had belonged to a woman who had survived the Holocaust by escaping to Spain after the rest of her family was killed.

In the house, Mannis found a small wooden box about the size of a backpack. It was a portable wine cabinet that the woman had bought in Spain. It had two doors carved with clusters of grapes, large hinges, and a small drawer at the bottom. It was made so that when one door was opened, so did the other and the drawer as well. A Jewish prayer was engraved on the back of the box. Mannis bought it.

Back in his shop, Mannis discovered that he didn't just get a box, but a box full of stuff. Inside were two wheat pennies from the 1920s, a lock of blond hair, a lock of dark hair, a small granite statue engraved with the word *shalom* (Hebrew for "peace"), a dried rosebud, a golden wine cup, and a cast-iron candle holder with legs shaped like octopus tentacles.

The contents were mysterious, but they're pretty much irrelevant to the story. What is relevant is that bad things started happening after Mannis acquired the box. His shop got trashed, and he started seeing shadowy forms, smelling ammonia, and having nightmares of a hag. Everyone he tried to give or sell the box to gave it back, including his mother, who suffered a stroke after he gifted it to her. Eventually, Mannis put it together that the source of all this strangeness was the dybbuk box.

Stories like this usually end with the owner dying, or with the object disappearing or winding up in a museum, but this story took a twist that could only be possible in the modern digital world. In 2003, Mannis posted the dybbuk box for sale on eBay, which at that time had been online for about eight years. In his description of the item, he went into extreme detail about his suspicions concerning the box and admitted that he was hoping somebody more knowledgeable than he about the paranormal could take it off his hands. He didn't

שלום
ONE CENT
ONE CENT

even put a reserve price on it. The beat-up old box full of strange ritualistic items sold for $140.

The buyer was a college student in Missouri named Iosif Nietzke. Whether Nietzke was an expert in cursed objects or Jewish ghosts, or wanted it for the story or – heck – to store wine is unclear. What is clear is what he recounted happening to him after winning the high bid on the dybbuk box.

According to Nietzke, he and his roommates began to experience various annoyances such as having sudden allergy-like symptoms, detecting strange smells, struggling through extended periods of torpor, and noticing their electronic devices dying often. Those strange happenings eventually escalated to hair loss and visions of dark, blurry things.

In an interesting twist on the trope of sending something dangerous back from whence it came, Nietzke listed the dybbuk box on eBay again, complete with the new story of his experiences. This was in 2004, less than a year after he won the box. This time it sold for $280.

The third buyer was Jason Haxton. He was the director of the Museum of Osteopathic Medicine at A. T. Still University in Missouri. Haxton claimed to have suffered various physical ills caused by the box, as well as receiving a big physical boost: he asserts that the box reversed the aging process for him, calling it his "fountain of youth." He kept it in an acacia wood box lined with 24-karat gold.

Haxton raised the profile of this wine cabinet stratospherically, writing a book about it in 2011, creating a website for the object, and discussing his paranormal purchase in interviews. He frames the chronicling of the box as a defense against the overwhelming number of requests for information he was getting about it once it was discovered that he was the owner.

The dybbuk box's reputation grew, and its story was fictionalized as a 2012 horror movie called *The Possession*, based in large part on a 2004 *Los Angeles Times* article about the box by Leslie Gornstein. The movie credits include a production consultant nod to Kevin Mannis, the owner who originally put the box on eBay.

In 2017, Zak Bagans, star of the paranormal reality TV show *Ghost Adventures*, bought it for his Haunted Museum in Las Vegas (for more on The Haunted Museum, see page 184). One source states that Bagans paid $10,000 for the Internet-famous box, a price that is in line with some other high-profile purchases for his museum. (Moral of the story: invest in cursed objects.)

The dybbuk box became the star of Bagans's museum. It's featured on the paper tickets alongside the words "the world's most haunted object." Inside, the box gets its own room, where it's displayed (and imprisoned) in a glass case under a spotlight and surrounded by a protective double ring of salt and dried sage. On my visit, the tour guide pointed out the place where the salt is disturbed and noted that the doors to the box have come ajar of their own accord. The gold-lined case Haxton kept it in is off to the side in its own glass case.

The final twist to the strange story involves the rapper Post Malone, who encountered the dybbuk box while guest-starring on an episode of Zak Bagans's *Ghost Adventures* in 2018. Subsequently, Post Malone suffered a series of high-profile misfortunes, including an emergency landing in a plane, a car accident, and a burglary. Not too long after, Bagans released infrared security footage showing Post Malone in the museum's dybbuk box room. The clip has no audio; in it, the rapper seems disturbed and eventually shoves Bagans out of the room. The implication was clear: Post Malone was the latest victim of the cursed dybbuk box.

Of course, another element of this story that's worth noting is that there was no such thing as a dybbuk box before Mannis's eBay listing. Sure, there were dybbuk folktales. And, sure, there were boxes. But Jewish mythology had no antecedent for this evil-genie-in-a-lamp-type story. In addition, a writer for *Skeptical Inquirer* magazine named Kenny Biddle has posited, and shown considerable evidence, that the box is too small to be a Jewish wine cabinet and is instead a minibar manufactured in New York in the mid-twentieth century. Oops. Still, that is no less strange a starting point than a Holocaust survivor's estate sale for the strange journey of this wooden box.

From an odd eBay listing to the silver screen to cursing one of the country's top music performers, the dybbuk box has ascended to pop culture infamy. As a result, there is always a dybbuk box for sale on eBay. So you could buy one today. If you dare.

The Basano Vase

PLACE OF ORIGIN:	MATERIAL:
ITALY	SILVER
AGE:	**CURRENT LOCATION:**
600 YEARS	UNKNOWN

This cursed silver vase from Italy is less a cursed object and more an out-and-out serial killer. It's been connected with about a dozen deaths beginning in the fifteenth century and ending sometime in the 1980s. And it has accomplished all that while holding many pretty bouquets of flowers along the way.

That is, if it even existed. Little evidence of the vase can be found, unless you count the dozens upon dozens of breathless blog posts and cursed object listicles. The story of the Basano Vase is remarkable for its singular lack of either verifiable facts or obvious falsehoods, both of which are entwined together throughout the history of any cursed object. If a cursed object has no names attached to it or doesn't come with believably specific narrative details, then some storyteller along the line is sure to make them up. And, yet, despite its lack of specific detail, the story of the cursed Basano Vase abides, always ready to jump into an Internet article about the most cursed objects in history with only a few paragraphs and a newspaper photo as evidence.

The story takes place in fifteenth-century Italy. It was the night before a wedding, and the bride-to-be had been given the silver vase as a wedding gift. Except that she's a bride-never-to-be. She was murdered before the ceremony, but by whom the story doesn't say. Her untimely death is sometimes ascribed to the cursed vase, and sometimes it's said that she cursed the vase as she died. Either way, the result is a cursed vase. The object stayed in the woman's family, killing relative after relative until someone realized the source of the misfortune and either hid the vase or had a priest hide it for them.

A vase with the power of death?

However that person hid the vase, they did a good job, because the trail went cold for five centuries before the vase was rediscovered in 1988. According to the lore, a man found it buried in his yard. There may or may not have been a note buried with it warning that death would find whoever owns it. Thinking that a fifteenth-century silver vase is probably pretty valuable, the finder auctioned it, eager to both rake in some cash and get the cursed object out of his house.

They say you never win an auction because the prize is that you lose a huge chunk of money. This maxim proved doubly true for the pharmacist who won the Basano Vase. He died months after the auction. As did the young doctor who bought the vase next. And the archeologist after that. The story recounts one more victim – no occupation listed this time – before a collector finally succumbed to the idea that cursed objects are real and the Basano Vase is one of them. The last owner threw the vase out a window, an admittedly untested method of ridding oneself of a cursed object.

A policeman witnessed the act and fined the collector for littering, while simultaneously attempting to return the vase. The collector took the fine, but not the vase. No museum in the city would take it, either. Word of the deaths associated with the vase had spread through the entire region, and folks had concluded that no flower arrangement is worth that cost. Finally, the vase disappeared, which is exactly how every cursed object story should end: with somebody wisely destroying it or hiding it forever. However, the Basano Vase story includes one more peculiar detail: that the silver vase was secreted inside a lead case, like it's radioactive instead of cursed.

With little evidence to back up the specifics, the story reads more like a fable than anything else, despite the fact that half of its events occurred during the Reagan administration. The one piece of evidence on the web that tethers the vase's legend to reality seems to be a single, cropped newspaper photo of a vessel with a rounded bottom and a collared top. It's almost heart-shaped, in the biological sense. The photo's caption and a few words from the article survived the image crop and appear to be in Croatian. The caption translates as: "Basano, a vase with the power of death?" The words from the article read something like: "The museum did not want!" The article might be the origin of the legend, based on real reporting, or it could be just another baton handoff of the legend in the Halloween edition of the paper, this time with a generic photo included by way of illustration. Unless a complete copy of the article is found, we'll never know.

The vase's name, Basano, is similarly a dead end. The word is a tense of the Italian verb *basare*, which means "to ground" or "to base." There is no place in Italy called Basano, and it doesn't seem to be a proper name. (*Bassano*, however, is part of the name of a city, Bassano del Grappo, where the Ponte Vecchio is located; it's also as a surname.)

So who knows? I considered banishing the Basano Vase from this book, as I banished other cursed objects where the word *rumored* refers to the object instead of the curse. But the vase's story is unusual in that it's not easily falsifiable, unlike, say, the story of the Woman of Lemb, another cursed object that often appears on lists with the Basano Vase. The story of that small stone figure includes several hard facts, including the name of the major museum that supposedly has it on display, which are so easily disproven that it quickly becomes apparent that there's no such thing as the Woman of Lemb.

But there's not enough information to outright discount the story of the Basano Vase, and I haven't been able to track it to its original source. Nevertheless, I include it here in case one day you find yourself in Italy and come across a great deal on an old, oddly shaped silver vase with a lead case thrown in for free. Just put it down and go get a gelato instead.

Rudolph Valentino's Ring

PLACE OF ORIGIN:
SAN FRANCISCO, CALIFORNIA

MATERIAL:
GOLD CIRCLET WITH A BROWN CAT'S-EYE STONE

NOTABLE OWNERS:
RUDOLPH VALENTINO, POLA NEGRI, RUSS COLUMBO, JOE CASINO, JACK DUNN

DEATH TOLL:
FIVE

His name was Rodolfo Alfonso Raffaello Pierre Filibert Guglielmi di Valentina d'Antonguolla. Film fans know him as Rudolph Valentino, one of the original stars of silent film in the 1920s. Paranormal fans know him for his cursed ring, which is said to have caused his death at age thirty-one and the subsequent deaths of nearly everyone who slipped a finger into its negative space afterward.

Valentino was born in 1895 in Italy and came to the United States at the age of eighteen to find a job. And, man, did he. Four years after arriving at Ellis Island he moved to the opposite coast to jump-start a movie acting career, back in the days when that was an experimental and somewhat disreputable career path. After a series of bit parts and bad-guy roles, Valentino quickly ascended the end credits to top billing. He was nicknamed "the Latin Lover" and accreted a rabid fan base. Upon his death, about one hundred grief-stricken admirers and curious onlookers clogged the Manhattan street surrounding his funeral. They say his death even caused a few suicides of people who didn't want to live in a Valentino-less world.

At some point, the A-lister picked up a ring in San Francisco. It was an ornate gold circlet bearing a large brown cat's-eye stone – sometimes called tiger's-eye – in its center. According to the story, the vendor advised Valentino against buying the ring because of all the harm it had inflicted on previous owners. But Valentino purchased it anyway. He hadn't crossed an ocean and climbed the heights of stardom in a burgeoning industry set to take over the world just to be told what he couldn't buy with his Hollywood paychecks.

In August 1926, Valentino was staying in Manhattan after the premiere of what would become his best-known movie, *The Son of the Sheik*, in which he played two roles, a father and son. He was in his room at the now-defunct Ambassador Hotel when he felt a pain in his gut. He was taken in for surgery for what turned out to be perforated stomach ulcers. These didn't kill him, though. He died about a week later from complications of the surgery. According to the story, he was wearing the ring at the time the pain started.

After his death, the ring went to Pola Negri, a Polish actress who had been romantically involved with Valentino in the past. She showed up at his funeral with her press agent, claimed that she was Valentino's fiancée, and sent a massive floral arrangement of red and white roses that spelled out her first name for the inevitable newspaper photos of the sad event. She also put on an Oscar-winning performance of grief that climaxed with her fainting atop Valentino's coffin. Soon after the ring came into her possession, Negri grew seriously ill. She eventually recovered and passed the ring on to its next victim, Russ Columbo.

Columbo, a handsome musician and singer known as "Radio's Valentino," seemed the perfect mark for his namesake's ring. And he indeed died under strange circumstances in 1934. He was shot in the face by Lansing Brown, a longtime friend of his. Brown testified that he was playing around with a firearm and a match, and the gun went off . . . into his friend. The death was ruled an accident.

Next, the ring went to a friend of Columbo's – one who didn't shoot him – named Joe Casino. He was hit and killed by a truck, and the ring passed hands to Casino's brother. Nothing bad happened to him, but that might be because the ring was stolen from his house by a burglar named James Willis. He set off an alarm during the break-in, and before he could flee, the police showed up and shot him dead. Valentino's ring was supposedly in his pocket.

The ring's fifth victim was a young actor named Jack Dunn, who was tapped to play Valentino in a biopic. After wearing the ring, Dunn contracted a blood disease and died before shooting even began.

Today, nobody knows where the ring is. Dunn was its last known victim. Rumor has it that Valentino's ring was hidden away in a safety deposit box in Los Angeles, not far from his final resting place in Hollywood Forever Cemetery. However, some say that it was stolen from said safety deposit box, so it may be even more missing than we think. And maybe that's a good thing.

As for the evidence that the ring existed in the first place, Valentino can be seen wearing a ring on his right pinky in the 1922 movie *The Young Rajah*, but it's difficult to see, and no one knows whether it belonged to him or was supplied by the costume department.

A possibly relevant ring appears in an oil painting by Spanish artist Federico Beltrán Masses, commissioned by Pola Negri after Valentino's death. The focal point of the painting is the rectangular brown stone on Negri's hand, spotlighted in the otherwise dim image that shows Valentino fading into navy-blue darkness, his eyes closed and his arms wrapped around a guitar.

But perhaps the best evidence of the cursed ring of Rudolph Valentino shows up in the catalog for his estate after his death. On page 81, among other rings of various stonage, is a short, innocent-looking entry for a "Honey Cats-Eye Ring." The word "cursed" doesn't appear in the copy.

Robert the Doll

PLACE OF ORIGIN:
GERMANY

DATE ACQUIRED:
EARLY 1900S

HEIGHT:
40 INCHES

NOTABLE OWNER:
ROBERT EUGENE OTTO

CURRENT LOCATION:
FORT EAST MARTELLO MUSEUM,
KEY WEST, FLORIDA

Every artist wants to achieve immortality. And Key West– based painter Robert Eugene Otto was more successful at it than most – except he doesn't live on through his art. His posthumous fame is the result of his cursed doll.

With dolls, there's often a thin line between cursed and haunted. Dolls personify curses a little bit more than other objects, and when a cursed object can stare back at you, it's a thousand times spookier. It may even make the curse rumors easier to believe. And that's the case with Robert the Doll.

Unlike most cursed and haunted dolls, Robert is one of a kind. It's about forty inches tall. It's stuffed with wood slivers called wood-wool, or excelsior, and dressed in an old sailor's uniform. Its eyes are black beads and its face is pockmarked with age, its features seemingly half formed, its mouth a lip-less pucker. It holds a stuffed lion under one arm and sits in a rocking chair. Nothing I'm telling you here is making it any less creepy, I know.

Forgive me!!!
WARNING
Dear Robert,
Sorry Robert!

The doll looked different, though, when a young Robert Eugene Otto was given it back in the early 1900s. Its face was originally painted like a clown's face. That sailor suit? Otto's own from when he was very young. Robert and Otto even share the same first name because Otto named the doll after himself. He went by Gene, however.

How Otto came to own Robert is not entirely clear. The story often goes that a housemaid gave it to him. She was either from the Bahamas or Jamaica, giving the story some island voodoo flair. Another version is that the doll was specially made for Otto and was even modeled on him. A third story has it that Otto's grandfather picked it up on a trip to Germany. This version, although the most prosaic, seems the mostly likely because the doll was indeed made in Germany.

Robert the Doll was created by the Steiff Company, a German-based toy maker that invented the teddy bear. In one version of the story, Robert was never meant to be a toy. Never meant for a child's love. Instead, it was a one-of-a-kind-doll specially made for a window display. Whether this is true or not, he's certainly one-of-a-kind now, more than a century after his creation.

Regardless of how the oversized doll came to Otto, the boy loved it. He dragged it with him everywhere. He talked to it at night and gave it a voice to talk back to him. He blamed it for mishaps. All innocent things kids do all the time but which take on a shade of the sinister considering how the story of Robert the Doll develops.

Little Gene held on to Robert the Doll even after he wasn't Little Gene anymore. It wasn't hard, because he also held on to his childhood home at 534 Eaton Street in Key West, Florida. His parents bought the house in 1898 and Otto lived there for most of his life, including the last forty years of it, along with his wife, pianist Annette Parker. Robert the Doll lived out that phase of his life in a turret in the house. Otto couldn't bear to get rid of him. He was like a reverse Dorian Gray painting up there, keeping his youthful dollness while his owner aged and grayed.

Otto died in 1974, and his wife died two years later. That's when the doll started getting spooky. People who lived in the house afterward would hear tiny running footsteps. They would hear a child's giggling. They swore the doll's expression changed. Eventually, one of the house's subsequent owners, Myrtle Reuter, got rid of Robert, banishing him to the Fort East Martello Museum in 1994. Meanwhile, the Otto home was renamed Artist House and is now a bed-and-breakfast that plays up its Victorian charm and adjacency to Old Town Key West.

The Fort East Martello Museum is located at 3501 South Roosevelt Boulevard in Key West. It's a Civil War era brick fort dating to 1862. It often features exhibits related to the history of the fort and that of the Key West area. It does some art shows. For a while the building itself was the most notable thing about the museum. Until it got Robert the Doll. Suddenly, Fort East Martello became a lot more interesting than the dozens of other historical forts that dot the East Coast.

Robert sits in a glass case in the middle of one of the rooms of the fort – a far cry from a child's bedroom. Maybe that's why it plays shenanigans on all the gawkers. Cameras malfunction. People see its head move or its face change expressions. Exactly what you expect a doll under glass to do. Robert exhibits all the telltale signs of a possessed or haunted object, and some people have wondered if the spirit of Otto himself is nestled deep in the doll's stuffing. But the most convincing evidence that the doll is cursed are the letters that come to the museum every single day for Robert.

They're not fan mail. They're apologies. Entreaties. Each letter represents a person looking to solve the misfortunes that began after they visited the doll and mocked it or photographed it without asking permission first. According to the letters, people have experienced flat tires upon leaving the museum. Some have suffered back aches, torn rotator cuffs, and fallen down stairs. Robert has been blamed for cancelled weddings, lost luggage, lost jobs, lost homes. Near-death experiences. Bankruptcy. The death of pets. Pretty much every bad thing under the Florida sun.

If you want the Robert experience without any of the risk, you can buy a one-third-scale replica of the doll in the museum gift shop. I have one. It's cuter at this smaller size. Less strange. Not at all creepy. Well, a little creepy. It usually sits on a shelf in my study, but I promoted it to my desk while I wrote this entry. He seemed to like the attention.

That Voodoo That You Do So Well

Some practices are shared by all people no matter their history or culture. Like cooking. And making music. And using little dolls to curse people. And when it comes to that last category, one cursed doll dominates them all: the voodoo doll.

Bound in popular consciousness to voodoo (or voudou, or hoodoo), a religion and folk practice from West Africa that the slave trade spread and splintered throughout the Caribbean and Louisiana, the voodoo doll is a makeshift human-shaped doll made of cloth, wax, or whatever's on hand. Voodoo dolls can be used to inflict curses in various ways, but the most popular is by sticking pins in them. Give your victim appendicitis by poking one in the doll's abdomen, afflict them with a migraine by taking a pin to the head, or kill them with a pin through the heart. It's much more satisfying than cursing a chair and hoping that the right person will take a seat.

However, attributing the voodoo doll to the practice of voodoo is a myth, a misinterpretation, a projection even, propagated by Europeans who were themselves obsessed with the practice. In European lore, witches used crude poppets made from cloth or sticks or vegetables to curse people. In Scotland, they used small "clay corpses" that dissolved under running water, along with the health of the victim. The practice traveled to the New World with the early European immigrants. The first person hanged in the Salem witch trials, Bridget Bishop, was accused of having a poppet made of rags and hog bristles.

The impulse behind using voodoo dolls is the same impulse behind burning effigies as political statements or destroying photos of your ex: Inflicting harm by proxy is extremely therapeutic.

Busby's Stoop Chair

PLACE OF ORIGIN: THIRSK, ENGLAND	**MATERIAL:** OAK
DATE OF CURSE: 1702	**CURRENT LOCATION:** THIRSK MUSEUM, NORTH YORKSHIRE, ENGLAND
CURSER: THOMAS BUSBY	

If you're bummed that you can't see the Baleroy Chair of Death (see page 98) for yourself, I've got good news. There's another cursed chair. And this one's on public display in England. Of the two, this chair is a little more intense, because it's killed as many as ten times more people and was cursed by a murderer right before he was executed.

The Thirsk Museum in North Yorkshire is dedicated to the history of the town of Thirsk. It's like many local museums – small and open seasonally and forced to compete with larger attractions like the popular World of James Herriot, which in this case is across the street.

The rooms of the museum contain the usual items of extremely local interest: furniture and clothing and toys, kitchenware, cricket stuff. Everyday items that illustrate the everyday lives in that everyday town. But it also houses a world-class treasure: the bones of the Saxon Giant. These remnants from a jaw and a foot dating to the sixth century were excavated from Castle Garth in Newcastle upon Tyne sometime in the 1990s. The bones belonged to a man who measured seven feet tall, making him a giant today and even more so back in his day, when average human heights were shorter.

But, although fascinating, the Saxon Giant isn't cursed. The chair nailed halfway up the wall is. This piece of oak furniture looks like a simple dining room chair, but its name belies its innocent appearance. Some call it Dead Man's Chair. Others the Chair of Death. Mostly, it's known as Busby's Stoop Chair, in honor of the man who supposedly cursed it before he was hanged for murder in 1702.

Thomas Busby was a counterfeiter, along with his partner Daniel Auty, in the town of Thirsk. As the story goes, Busby got into that shady business by marrying Auty's daughter Elizabeth. At some point the two men got into a fight, maybe about Auty's daughter, maybe about Auty sitting in Busby's favorite chair at his favorite pub (in some versions of the story, Busby owns the pub; in others he lodges there). Whatever the cause of the skirmish, it ended with a drunken Busby going to Auty's farmhouse on the outskirts of town and bashing in the other man's skull with a hammer. Busby was caught and sentenced to hang. On the way to the gallows, he asked if he could stop by the pub for a last draught of ale, which he was allowed. He sat in his regular seat, downed the drink, and then said, "May sudden death come to anyone who dare sit in my chair." If he was going to be strung up for murder, he might as well take a few more with him.

Busby was hanged, after which point his body was dipped

in tar to preserve it. It was strung from a stoop (or pole) as a caution to other would-be counterfeiters, murderers, and chair-cursers.

Eventually, the tragedy became a defining element of the town's history. The pub was renamed Busby Stoop Inn, and the cursed chair was used as a draw for the curious after Busby's body finally decayed.

It was all fun and games and criminal corpses until the cursed chair started to work. Supposedly, anybody who sits in the Busby Stoop Chair comes to a bad end. A chimney sweep hanged himself in 1894. Many soldiers from the nearby base went off to war and never came home. In 1967, two Royal Air Force pilots died in a car crash on their way home from the pub. A builder fell from a roof and died. A cleaner died of a brain tumor. A beer deliverer was killed in a crash. All because they chose the wrong seat at the bar.

These death stories continued all the way to the 1970s, at which point the pub's owner got too spooked by the chair and excommunicated it to the Thirsk Museum, about three miles away. The museum's staff hung it on a wall at roughly head height to ensure that nobody could drop an ass in it again.

Now, this being a curse story, it's going to have some holes. For instance, the records of the inciting incident are sparse. It's unknown if Busby married Auty's daughter, or if he murdered Auty. Back then, counterfeiting was a crime punishable by death, so all that cursing and hanging and tarring could have been about a handful of fake coins.

But these are mere plot holes. The giant tear in the story of this cursed object comes courtesy of Dr. Adam Bowett, a furniture historian. In a 2014 article in the local daily newspaper the *Northern Echo*, Bowett stated that upon examination, he concluded that the chair hanging from the wall of the Thirsk Museum has machine-made parts. That means it was made sometime after 1840 – about a century and a half after the events that supposedly caused the curse.

This unfortunate finding could mean that the story around this cursed object is completely fabricated. But I like to think otherwise. I like to think that the inn accidentally gave the Thirsk Museum the wrong chair. And because that inn still stands on Busby Stoop Road (although as of this writing it's an Indian restaurant called the Jaipur Spice), the real Busby Stoop Chair has remained in the building for the past half century, quietly killing people who just wanted to have a drink or a curry.

The Conjured Chest

PLACE OF ORIGIN:
KENTUCKY

DATE MADE:
CIRCA 1830

CREATOR:
REMUS, A SLAVE

CURRENT LOCATION:
KENTUCKY HISTORICAL SOCIETY, FRANKFORT, KENTUCKY

NUMBER OF VICTIMS:
SIXTEEN

It's a nice old chest of drawers. Hand-carved polished mahogany. Elegant scrollwork and leaf details. Almost four feet tall. Antique. Convenient little casters on its legs. And on the front of each of its four drawers is an old-fashioned keyhole for an old-fashioned key. If you saw it in an antiques shop or at an estate sale, it would be a great find. The only problem is that you can't put anything in its drawers. Whoever owns the items placed within will come to great harm – or may even die. Which kind of defeats the purpose of a chest of drawers, but cursed objects aren't generally known for their utility.

The curse attached to this piece of furniture dates all the way back to its creation, around 1830, when it was crafted for a wealthy and cruel Kentucky slaveowner named Jeremiah Graham. The "devil incarnate" was what one of his descendants called him. Graham commanded one of his enslaved workers, Remus, to build a chest of drawers for his imminent firstborn, which Remus did. But for some reason Graham hated the chest, so much that he beat Remus to death.

The other slaves in the household banded together to retaliate. They sprinkled dried owl's blood inside the chest while reciting a spell called a "dirge of conjure." They cursed it, and thus it became known as the Conjured Chest. The chest would torment Graham's descendants over the course of the next century, killing or harming as many as sixteen people.

The chest was placed in the nursery of Graham's firstborn, and the child's clothes filled its drawers. That child soon died. Victim number two was Graham's nephew. The Conjured Chest was moved to his room at some point after his cousin's death. He filled the drawers with his clothes and survived childhood, but was stabbed to death by a servant at age twenty-one.

The Conjured Chest was eventually moved to Tennessee to furnish the house of Graham's daughter, Catherine Winchell, who had eloped there. Not long after it arrived, however, her husband, John Ryan, left to find work in New Orleans and Catherine died of an illness in short succession. A week later, Ryan followed suit when he was smashed in the head by the stage plank of a boat. Their daughter Eliza and her husband, John David Gregory, inherited the chest.

Their daughter, Louise, died at age ten after using the chest. Their daughter-in-law, Stella Stonecipher, died within two years of putting her wedding clothes in the chest. Later, a relative of the Gregory family, Mable Louis Whitehead, moved in with Eliza and married a man named Wilbur Harlan. Four years later, they had a baby boy named Chester, who died at two weeks old after his clothes went into the chest. Wilbur died only a few years later for the same reason.

John David Gregory's sister, Lucy Gregory, knitted her son Emmet a pair of gloves and a scarf as a Christmas gift. She hid the present in one of the drawers of the Conjured Chest. Her son never received the gift, because that December he fell thirty feet through a train trestle to his death.

The curse continued to wreak havoc in Eliza's life. Her daughter Nellie Gregory's wedding dress was stashed in the chest after her wedding, and her husband soon left her. And then John David Gregory died. Eliza took her own life after that – becoming an indirect victim of the curse.

The chest would torment Graham's descendants over the course of the next century, killing or harming as many as sixteen people.

The chest then came into the possession of Eliza's granddaughter, Virginia Cary Hudson, the great-great-granddaughter by marriage of Jeremiah Graham. Hudson is a pivotal figure in this story, and the reason we know about the Conjured Chest at all. She's the one who wrote down the tragic chain of events that befell her relatives who just wanted a place to store their clothes. According to Hudson, she heard the story of the chest as a child from her grandmother, the tragic Eliza, and saw the curse proved true when she witnessed several relatives suffer.

Hudson's first child was born prematurely and died after she placed the baby's clothes in the chest. Her second daughter, Ann, was inflicted with polio and suffered symptoms from it for her entire life, after her clothes were placed in the chest. Wilbur Brister, the husband of Hudson's third daughter (also named Virginia), died from an overdose of ether during an appendectomy after his wife's wedding clothes were placed in the chest. A neighbor set his hunting clothes in the chest and was killed in a gun accident. And Hudson's son was stabbed in the hand at school after his clothes were stored in the chest.

Hudson turned to a family servant named Sallie for advice. Sallie knew how to get rid of such a curse and told Hudson exactly how to do it. First, she instructed Hudson to get a dead owl, though one that was given to her without her asking for it. Fortunately, somebody had gifted Hudson a taxidermized owl in the past. The other ingredient was leaves from a willow tree planted by a friend, because, Sallie said, "willows mean sorrow." Fortunately, Hudson knew where one of those was, too. She drove to the tree and plucked sixteen leaves from its boughs, one for each family member who had been affected by the curse, and then a few more just in case.

She took the owl, set it up on the stove, and, under its glassy watchful eye, boiled the batch of willow leaves in a black pot from dawn to nightfall. After that, she took the concoction, bottled it in a jug, and buried it under a lilac bush ("flowers mean love and promise," said Sallie), with the handle of the jug facing east, because, Sallie said, "the sun comes from the East and the devil hates light."

Sallie told Hudson that she would know that the curse was broken if somebody in the household died before the leaves on the flowering bush dropped. Sallie died a few months later.

Hudson went on to become a *New York Times* best-selling author of books of essays and letters about Southern life in the early twentieth century. All the quotes in this entry appear in her essay "Mama Relates the Tale of a Conjured Chest" in the book *Flapdoodle, Trust & Obey* (Harper & Row, 1966). But they weren't published until about a decade after her death in 1954, when her daughter, Virginia C. Mayne, decided to show them to the world.

But while Mayne made her mother's words public, she remained private about her mother's cursed chest of drawers. She hid it in the attic for decades and made sure that no clothes were placed inside of it.

In 1976, the chest finally left the family when Mayne donated it to the Kentucky History Museum in Frankfort. In 2017, she published a short book about it called *The Conjured Chest: A Cursed Family in Old Kentucky*, in which she explains that her mother, in her books, had used pseudonyms for all the family members. Mayne laid out the real names and relations of the victims of the Conjured Chest, which I have used here.

The Conjured Chest is owned by the Kentucky Historical Society to this day, although it's rarely displayed. The owl feathers from the original countercharm still rest in the top drawer.

The Conjured Chest illustrates a particularly insidious element of cursed object lore. When the object is so ordinary and so mundanely useful, that's when it's most harmful. Because no matter how much misfortune befalls your family, you'll probably never suspect the chest of drawers.

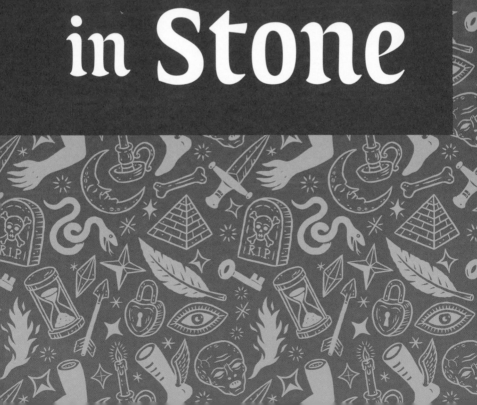

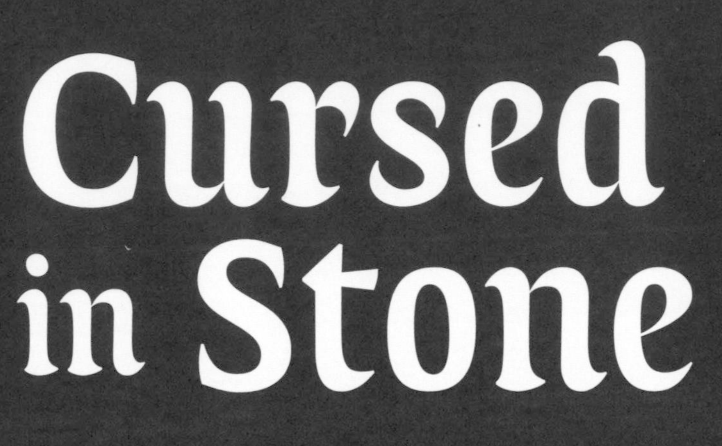
Cursed
in Stone

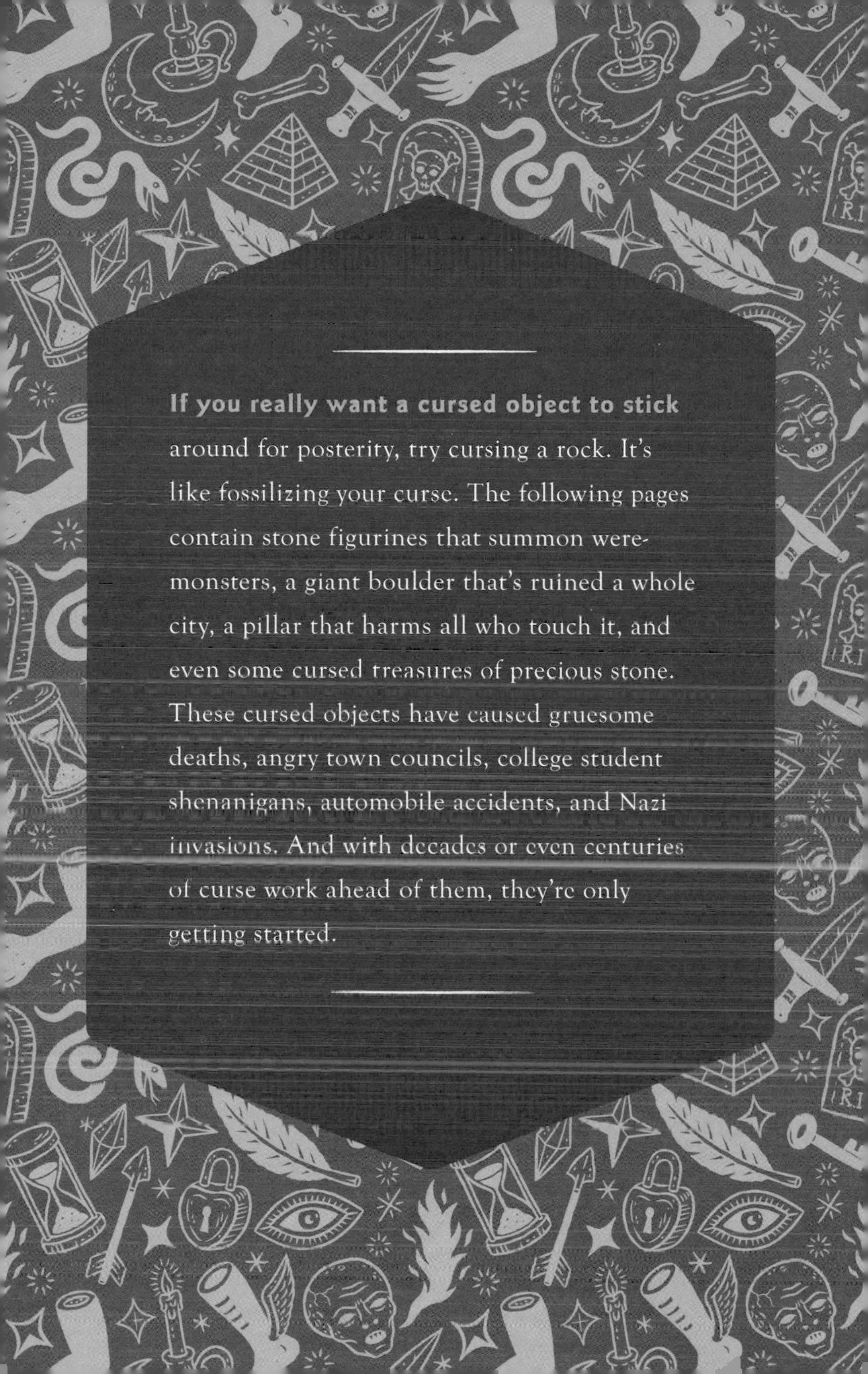

If you really want a cursed object to stick around for posterity, try cursing a rock. It's like fossilizing your curse. The following pages contain stone figurines that summon were-monsters, a giant boulder that's ruined a whole city, a pillar that harms all who touch it, and even some cursed treasures of precious stone. These cursed objects have caused gruesome deaths, angry town councils, college student shenanigans, automobile accidents, and Nazi invasions. And with decades or even centuries of curse work ahead of them, they're only getting started.

The Little Mannie with His Daddy's Horns

PLACE OF ORIGIN:	MATERIAL:
WEST AFRICA	FELSITE
DATE DISCOVERED:	**CURRENT LOCATION:**
1960S	MANCHESTER MUSEUM, MANCHESTER, ENGLAND

Sometimes we give spooky things silly names to make them seem less spooky. Sometimes it works. Sometimes it makes them even spookier. Let me tell you about Little Mannie, and you can make the call on this particular cursed object.

Little Mannie is a bulbous, carved stone figure about three inches tall. Viewed straight-on, he looks like a bald man with an oversized head, heavy brow, large nostrils, and nubby arms or wings jutting out from a small, legless trunk. Looking at him in profile reveals faint arcs on the side of his head that some describe as horns. From that angle, his nose is more snoutlike, making him look ram-headed and giving him a somewhat occultic appearance, which may be the inspiration behind his full name: The Little Mannie with His Daddy's Horns.

A. J. N. W. Prag, who worked at the Manchester Museum at England's University of Manchester, gives a detailed, first-hand account of the artifact in the 2015 book *The Materiality of Magic*, edited by Ceri Houlbrook and Natalie Armitage. According to him, Little Mannie was found in the 1960s by a cleaning lady named Lucy Healy underneath the Conservative Club in Hollingworth, England. While vigorously washing the dirt floor of the basement of the seventeenth-century building, she unearthed a small lump of stone. The figure was originally painted green, but, in the ardor of her cleaning, she had removed the paint. Healy decided that she wanted to hang onto the figure.

After its discovery became common knowledge in the town, a local history professor named Tony Ward and his friend Pat Ellison conducted an amateur dig at the spot. They discovered a ritualistic arrangement of artifacts. A circle of candles surrounded chicken and rabbit bones, ivory billiard counters, and the statue of a motherlike figure. It seemed it was part of a foundation sacrifice, meant to bring luck to the house. Word got around, and Little Mannie started to get locally famous.

In 1974, the item came to the attention of A. J. N. W. Prag, who was putting together an exhibit of Celtic heads for the Manchester Museum. Celtic heads are small stone faces with simplistic features that seem to pop up anywhere in Europe where the Celts lived, especially the United Kingdom. They are often thousands of years old. The region where Little Mannie was found had yielded quite a few Celtic heads, so Prag was intrigued by the figure.

Although Little Mannie's design seemed different from that of the other carved Celtic heads, it was determined to be close enough to get lumped into the category, especially since the going hypothesis was that it represented the horned Celtic god Cernunnos, the lord of animals.

Prag tried to buy the stone figure from Healy, but she wouldn't sell it for many years. In the mid-1980s, Prag was finally able to acquire it. The Healys needed the money for a vacation and, it seemed, had been suffering a series of minor misfortunes since bringing the figure into their house.

After Little Mannie arrived at the Manchester Museum, staff also began to suffer minor misfortunes. The staff member who photographed Little Mannie for archiving dinged his car twice in consecutive nights, after eighteen years with a perfect driving record. A director broke a thumb after scoffing at the piece. An exhibit worker gashed open his head. Other accounts of minor sickness and damage and harm swirled around Little Mannie over the years, until it became infamous at the museum and many members of the staff decided to keep their distance. At first, the museum geologist wouldn't even examine it to determine what stone it was made of.

At some point, Pat Ellison, one of the amateur excavators, visited the museum to see the figure. After hearing about all the mischief it seemed to be causing, she took it in her lap and stroked it before pulling a few strands of hair from her head and wrapping Little Mannie in them to deactivate its powers. Or to make it happy and less inclined to cause misfortune. One of the two.

One night Prag took Little Mannie home so that he could take him to London to show him to a materials expert. That evening somebody broke Prag's car window, and the next morning, while in the bathroom on the train to London, his zipper broke and he had to safety-pin his pants shut. On July 2, 1991, *The Sun* ran a piece on this incident under the headline, "There's No Flies on Little Mannie: Curse Rips Boss's Zip." The headline font dripped ominously.

That same year, during Little Mannie's first public exhibition, an expert in African artifacts examined Little Mannie and informed museum staff that the figure was unequivocally a *nomoli* statue from Sierra Leone. Nomoli are ancient carved figures from an unnamed extinct civilization. They are often discovered underground or in caves throughout the area. The Mende people of Sierra Leone use these artifacts today to protect their homes and bless their crops, often by burying them. So nomoli are good luck charms, the exact opposite of cursed objects.

When you compare photos of nomoli with images of Little Mannie, the theory seems unassailable, especially when you compare them both to Celtic heads. Little Mannie looks exactly like a weathered, broken version of the African figurines. When the stone that Little Mannie was carved from was finally examined, it was found to be felsite, which is plentiful in both England and Western Africa.

As for how a nomoli figure traveled more than 4,000 miles only to wind up buried beneath an old house, a few theories exist. But they all boil down to trade of one sort or another. I mean, it's England — they've been ransacking the world's artifacts for centuries. But it could also explain how a good luck charm could go bad, by being removed from home and buried in a strange land.

As for *why* it was buried there, among the chicken bones and ivory, is much harder to imagine and will likely remain a mystery.

Today, you can find Little Mannie buried in a drawer at the Discovery Centre of the Manchester Museum. If you look closely, you might see Pat Ellison's hair still wrapped around him. Whether it pacified him or not is up for debate.

The Cursing Stone

ARTISTS:
GORDON YOUNG,
ANDY ALTMAN

TEXT BY:
GAVIN DUNBAR,
ARCHBISHOP OF GLASGOW

YEAR INSTALLED:
2003

CURRENT LOCATION:
CARLISLE, ENGLAND

The story of the Cursing Stone of Carlisle, England, should be a straightforward one. It's a stone with a curse engraved on its surface. Sounds pretty standard for a cursed object, right? But it's actually a weird story, one that has both ancient and contemporary chapters, is rooted in history and art and tragedy and superstition, and illustrates, perhaps better than any other entry in this book, how powerful the concept of a cursed object is for us imaginative apes.

The story starts in the latter centuries of Europe's medieval period. The constant warring between England and Scotland created a border zone that was inhospitable to the English and Scottish farmers who call that borderland home. So those farmers beat their plowshares into swords and became *reivers* (or raiders). These border reivers were born of violence, and they caused even more, donning light armor, picking up lances and bows and shields, mounting horses, and plundering both Scot and Sassenach alike. Things got so bad, there was talk among the English of repairing Hadrian's Wall, a defensive fortification built about 1,400 years earlier by the Roman Empire.

And though the reivers pissed off a lot of people, no one was angrier than Gavin Dunbar, the Archbishop of Glasgow. In 1525, he penned a 1,069-word curse against the reivers and had it read in churches all over the island. Here's a snippet:

> I denounce, proclaim and declare to all and sundry, that the committing of the said pointless murders and slaughtering of innocents, burnings, cattle rustling, plundering, thefts and despoiling; both openly in the daylight and under silence of night, as well as within Church property and on Church land; together with their partakers, assistants, suppliers, knowing receivers of their persons, the goods burnt and stolen by them, or any part thereof, and the counsellors and defenders of their evil deeds are generally cursed,

loathed, detested, denounced and collectively cursed with the great cursing.

The full text of that "great cursing" is too long to include here, but here's a summary (which is also almost too long to include here): Dunbar started by cursing every part of their bodies, from the hair on their heads to the soles of their feet and all parts inside and outside their skin. Then he cursed all of their activities – riding, standing, drinking, basically everything that a body can do. Next, he cursed their homes and their families. Everything they owned. Everywhere they lived.

He then cursed them with every curse ever recorded in the Bible. From Lucifer getting kicked out of heaven to Adam getting kicked out of Eden, from the slaying of Abel to the drowning of the world in Noah's day. Sodom and Gomorrah, the Tower of Babel, the plagues of Egypt, the curse of Judas, and every other Old and New Testament horror.

He then severed the reivers from heaven and all human contact and from the church. Finally, he ended his curse by consigning them all to the fiery pit with Lucifer and his buds. You'll be hard-pressed to find a longer or more thorough curse.

But this isn't a book about curses. It's a book about cursed objects. And we're getting to that. Eventually, England and Scotland figured things out and the reivers went back to farming and eventually became romanticized like outlaws in the Wild West of America and the pirates of the seven seas.

Cut to 2001. To celebrate the newly minted millennium, an artist named Gordon Young was commissioned to design a piece of public art in Carlisle, England, which is right on the border with Scotland.

For that piece of turn-of-the-millennium art, Young found inspiration in the long-gone reivers, both because Carlisle was in the borderland that spawned them and because Young himself traced his lineage back to the reivers. Andy Altman, who was charged with building Young's design, took a 14-ton rounded granite rock the size of a wardrobe, polished it up, and inscribed 383 of the 1,069 words of Gavin Dunbar's curse on its surface. He then placed it on a floor of tiles with reiver family surnames engraved in them — Simpson, Nixon, Blackadder, Radcliffe, and a few dozen others. He gave the piece a matter-of-fact name: *Cursing Stone and Reiver Pavement*. It was a relatively inoffensive piece of art reflecting an interesting part of British history in the place where it occurred . . . until it became more than that.

In 2003, Young's piece was placed in a walking tunnel under the main road connecting the Tullie House Museum and Art Gallery to Carlisle Castle, which was erected two centuries before the first reiver dropped his barley for a bow. A week after its installation, local livestock were hit by a furious case of foot-and-mouth disease, killing half of the cattle. Cow corpses were piled high and burned in pyres to stop the illness from spreading. Factories closed and people lost jobs. Less than four years after the installation of the Cursing Stone, the nearby River Eden flooded, submerging thousands of houses for days. The local football team, Carlisle United, even got relegated to a lower division. It was an Egypt-level spate of plagues.

And people started to blame that rock. All because it had a curse engraved on it. Even if the curse wasn't aimed at the people of Carlisle. Even if only a small section of the curse appeared on the stone. Even if it was only an art project. I mean, its name is the Cursing Stone – people needed something to blame for all their grief, and Gordon Young's rock seemed the best target. There were even accusations that Satanists were using it as an altar.

The murmuring and finger-pointing became so widespread that the local council mulled over the prospect of moving or destroying the Cursing Stone. One of the more vocal proponents of these options, a council member named Jim Tootle, died suddenly at the age of fifty-nine.

But that's not why the council didn't move it. They decided that doing so would be cost-prohibitive. Still, they had to do something. So they had a Bible verse inscribed behind the rock to act as a counter-curse. It was Philippians 4:8–9. And after that, nothing bad happened in Carlisle ever again, I guess. Or at least people stopped blaming the rock.

As for Gordon Young's take on the curse? The football-loving artist told the *Guardian* in 2005, "If I thought my sculpture would have affected one Carlisle United result, I would have smashed it myself years ago."

The Monogram of Patrick Hamilton

CURRENT LOCATION:	SITE COMMEMORATION:
ST. SALVATOR'S CHAPEL, UNIVERSITY OF ST. ANDREWS, ST. ANDREWS, SCOTLAND	MARTYRDOM OF PATRICK HAMILTON
	YEAR OF HAMILTON'S DEATH: 1528

Set into the cobblestoned path outside the large arched doorway of a chapel at the oldest college in Scotland is a monogram crafted out of stone tiles. In it, the hump of a *P* welts inward from the top left stem of an *H*. At first glance, one might guess that the melded PH is the logo of the school. Maybe the mark of a school founder or a wealthy donor. You could imagine that monogram stitched in expensive thread onto a crisp golf polo or etched into the glass doors of a financial company.

But they are the initials of a saint. They are installed on the site where he burned for six hours. And they are cursed.

The University of St. Andrews was established in 1410 in the town of St. Andrews on the east coast of Scotland. Its long history began during a time of religious and political tumult in Europe. The charter of the university was awarded by an exiled pope during the Great Occidental Schism, when Catholics found themselves governed by multiple popes simultaneously.

About a century later, the college became a place of both learning and burning during the Protestant Reformation, thanks to Martin Luther nailing his theses to a church door in Germany and sparking a holy war in Christianity that vastly increased the number of saints and martyrs. At the nearby St. Andrews Castle, Protestants were imprisoned in its infamous bottle dungeon (a claustrophobically thin, vertical chamber that prisoners were lowered into through a small hole in the ceiling), with relief coming only at the end of a rope or on a fiery stake.

For one example, in 1546 Archbishop David Beaton ordered the martyrdom of Protestant preacher George Wishart via strangulation and burning, and then became a Catholic martyr himself when he was killed in retaliation. Beaton's corpse was hung out a window of the castle for the entire town to see before being preserved in pickle brine. It was not a great time to be God-fearin'.

Today there are monuments to martyrs throughout the town of St. Andrews, but of all those memorials, the PH in front of St. Salvator's Chapel is the most ominous. Built in 1450, the Gothic St. Salvator's Chapel is still in use as a campus chapel and is referred to on its website as the "medieval heart of the University of St. Andrews." But on your way in, you have to avoid that monogram in the cobblestones. At least, if you're a student of the university.

The PH stands for Patrick Hamilton, and he was the first Scottish Protestant martyr of many. Hamilton was born in 1504 and studied abroad in France and Belgium, where he became enamored by the reforms of Martin Luther. He brought these new ideas with him when he returned home and joined the University of St. Andrews. Preaching that kind of stuff in a then-Catholic school and country got him into trouble, so he fled to Germany for a few months.

Upon his return to Scotland, Hamilton got married but didn't settle down. He kept preaching and writing about Luther's new doctrines. In February 1528, at the age of twenty-four, he was hauled before Archbishop James Beaton – the uncle of David Beaton – convicted of being a heretic, and executed that day. Hamilton's trial was attended by none other than Gavin Dunbar, the Archbishop of Glasgow, who three years earlier wrote a 1,069-word curse against the border reivers that inspired Gordon Young's Cursing Stone (see page 139). Dunbar signed Hamilton's execution papers.

It was a long day. The executioners chose a spot outside the doors of St. Salvator's Chapel and created a pyre of wood, coals, and gunpowder. Due to some bad winds, the fire was more fickle than usual, and it took a long time to catch

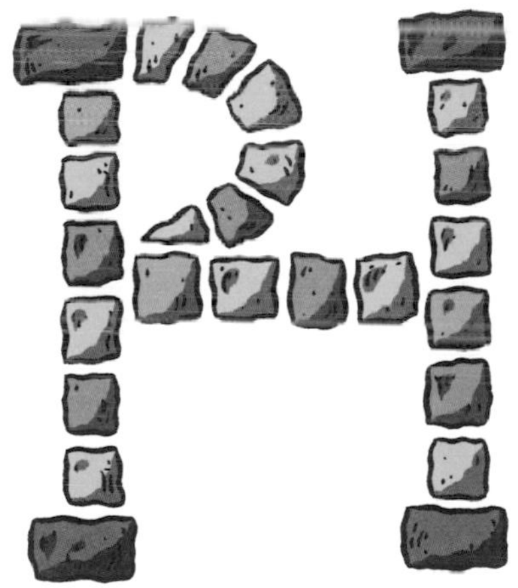

reliably. As a result, the heretic-burning ran from noon until six o'clock, an agonizing six hours for Hamilton, before they finally and mercifully achieved the temperature at which Protestants burn. Hamilton said a lot in those six hours, including responding to the taunts of friars in the crowd by calling one of them a "messenger of Satan" and another a "wicked man." He also refused to recant, and history has recorded his final words as, "Lord Jesus, receive my spirit," which were among the final words of the martyred Saint Stephen before he was stoned to death in the book of Acts.

Unlike Saint Stephen, whose final, final words were to ask forgiveness for his killers, Hamilton is said to have finished by bringing down a curse upon the university. The exact words of that curse are lost, but the actual effects of the curse are known. And they're sort of gentle, especially since they are supposedly born out of such a violent ending. Basically, any student of St. Andrews who steps upon that spot marked today by the PH . . . will fail their final exams. That's it. That's the curse.

But it's a curse that's become engrained in campus culture. Even the university webpage for the historic chapel shows a closeup photo of a student's boots leaping over the letters. However, failing exams is a big deal for students, and fortunately the lore includes a few remedies for the student who accidentally treads upon the martyr site. Some say to reverse the curse, you need to run around the quad eight times backwards — and possibly naked. Others say you need to participate in the school's annual May Day Dip, when the students dive naked and seminaked into the cold North Sea at sunrise. Turns out nudity breaks curses — at least in college.

And if you think a couple of letters in a sidewalk aren't

all that eerie, you're not wrong. But that's because I haven't told you about the spookiest element of the story and possibly the entire inspiration for the curse: the creepy charred face. If you look up at the side of St. Salvator's Chapel, looming over the site of Patrick Hamilton's death is a single brick carved with an angry-looking face that is blackened, as if it had been burned. It's an embellishment left over from the chapel's much more ornate Catholic days, before the Protestants stripped it down to their liking. The ancient countenance stares down at the spot of the tragedy, as if the ghost of Patrick Hamilton is overseeing and relishing the work of his curse. Or maybe he's just angry that the result of his curse isn't more profound.

The Cursed Pillar

PLACE OF ORIGIN:	INCARNATIONS:
AUGUSTA, GEORGIA	THREE
YEAR CREATED:	YEARS DESTROYED:
1830	1935, 1958, 2016

At the south corner of Fifth and Broad streets in Augusta, Georgia, is a historical sign, the kind that you can find in any state in the country in various state-specific color schemes and usually on the sides of roads. This sign in Augusta is green and yellow, and it tells the tale of a nearby stone pillar that was cursed by a traveling preacher. But there is no pillar to be seen, and that's because this is the rare cursed object that cursed itself.

In 1830, a large city bazaar called the Lower Market was erected in the area where the sign now stands. It replaced another market building that had burned down the previous year. At some point, a preacher (the historical sign calls the man a "wandering 'exhorter'") used it as an impromptu church, shouting about the terrors of hell and the glories of salvation beneath its roof. Those who were just there to sell their fruits and veggies and cows and sheep got annoyed, and he was removed from the premises. But not before he put a curse on the place.

As he was dragged out, the preacher added one more diatribe to his sermon. He swore that because of the hard-heartedness of the hijacked audience, the market would be destroyed by a furious wind from the Almighty, until all that was left was a single stone pillar, the same one that the wandering exhorter was standing by. It's a variation on the Biblical Samson story, in which Samson, an Israelite leader who had been captured and blinded by his Philistine enemies, was granted superhuman power by God to pull an entire Philistine temple down by its pillars using his bare hands. In 1878, the market was indeed destroyed by what the historical sign calls a "freakish tornado," and all that was left of it was a single stone pillar.

A variation on the story is that the preacher didn't come around until after the destruction of the Lower Market and that he set up his soapbox beside the freestanding pillar. His curse in this version? That if anyone tore down that pillar, lightning would kill them.

In a third variation, the Lower Market, despite no historical substantiation to back this up, was a slave market, and the pillar was a whipping and chaining post. Eventually, a slave with the power of voodoo at their beckon cursed the market, causing its destruction. The pillar survived, the remnants of the curse lingering within its stone and mortar.

All three curse stories end with the survival of the tall, freestanding column called the Cursed Pillar, also known as the Haunted Pillar and the Killer Pillar. It was ten feet tall and made of concrete-covered brick. That past tense is on purpose. More on that in a minute.

Over the years, the curse story has broadened its reach. It's said that anybody who merely touched the pillar could fall victim to the curse. Highway workers just doing their jobs around the pillar have supposedly been felled by the death curse. People in pickups trucks loaded with tow chains and fueled by vendettas against the pillar are rumored to have died in car accidents en route to take it down. They even say that the intersection at which it's placed sees a higher-than-usual number of accidents.

But nobody has gotten it worse than the pillar itself. It has been destroyed three different times. And each time, a vehicle was involved.

The first time it happened was in 1935. Few details survive of the accident, but the *Augusta Chronicle* acknowledged the driver escaped unhurt, while the pillar was "reduced . . . to a pile of brick and cement."

For some reason, the pillar was rebuilt, although it was moved to a slightly more protected location nearby. And I say *slightly* because in 1958, on a Friday the thirteenth, a giant bale of cotton probably weighing some five or six hundred pounds fell off a passing truck and demolished the pillar again.

And, for some reason, despite the fact that the accident presumably freed the people of Augusta from the curse, the pillar was rebuilt a second time, and this time moved even further back from the road. But the pillar really must have been cursed, because in December 2016, it was completely destroyed by a car.

A gray Ford Taurus bounced off a truck and barreled directly into the Cursed Pillar. Photos of the carnage immediately circulated on social media, showing the pillar lying on the ground, the cement coating stripped, and the brick entrails underneath scattered across the sidewalk. People grabbed pieces of it as souvenirs. GoFundMe pages were set up. Overall, people seemed sad to see it go, in spite of the curse.

As of the writing of this book, the pillar has not been rebuilt, despite promises by local groups to do so and despite the still-standing historical sign. But chances are the Cursed Pillar will rise again.

Why does the city of Augusta keep resurrecting such a supernaturally dangerous object? The truth can probably be traced to 1931, decades after the destruction of the market and only a handful of years before the first destruction of the pillar. The mayor at the time, William Jennings, hired a press agent to market the curse. That's right. The curse has always been about tourism. That's why ghost tours swung by the pillar. That's why every day, local shopkeepers witnessed tourists touching and even hugging the pillar. Once account even reported somebody pissing on it.

But I like to think of it differently. Perhaps tourism is only a pretense for this push for preservation. After all, the city has far more bankable attractions. Like the Augusta National Golf Club, host of the Masters, one of the most important golf tournaments in the history of the sport. It's also the birthplace of James Brown and Hulk Hogan and Lawrence Fishburne.

Maybe Augustans ritually and dutifully rebuild the Cursed Pillar because they are terrified of what might happen if they don't take care of it. Maybe the city is always the width of a stack of bricks and cement away from tragedy. And maybe they better rebuild it soon.

No Cursed Stone Unreturned

Most of the rocks in the national parks and heritage sites of the world are cursed. Seriously. The stones of Blarney Castle in County Cork, Ireland, are all cursed. As is the volcanic rock and pumice of Hawaii Volcanoes National Park on the Big Island. The stones at Australia's Uluṟu-Kata Tjuṯa National Park, home to the giant sandstone monolith known both as Uluru and as Ayers Rock, are all cursed. So is the stone-like fossilized wood of Petrified Forest National Park near Holbrook, Arizona. And these are just a few examples.

The thing is, these cursed stones don't activate unless visitors remove them from the park and take them home as souvenirs. As long as they stay at the heritage site, they're just dots on the landscape. But the second the rocks leave the park, they bring misfortune to whoever's backpacks they're in.

While these curse stories sound suspiciously like psychological damage control propagated by park authorities, the truth is that almost every day these parks receive packages from tourists who ignored the warnings and took a rock home. These packages usually include both the pilfered rock and an apologetic letter explaining that the second the person returned home from their trip with their stolen stone, bad things started happening to them.

So next time you're at a national park or heritage site with important stones, maybe go to the gift shop instead.

The Hexham Heads

PLACE OF ORIGIN:	CURRENT LOCATION:
HEXHAM, ENGLAND	UNKNOWN
YEAR MADE:	MATERIAL:
1956	CONCRETE

I'm going to give you the moral of the story up front for this one: be careful what you dig up in your garden; you may unleash werewolves. I'll also give you its secondary moral: be careful what you stake your academic reputation on; a construction worker may fool you.

In 1971, two young brothers, Colin and Leslie Robson, were digging in their garden at 3 Rede Avenue in the town of Hexham, England. The boys unearthed two small stone heads – rough, skull-like, and each about two and a half inches tall. The features of the two heads were different, but both seemed primitive, maybe a little creepy, and certainly strange. The heads had short stems on them, as if they'd been broken off at the neck from larger artifacts.

However, digging up tiny stone heads is not that uncommon in the United Kingdom. They're called Celtic heads and are generally thought to be ornaments that have broken off from other objects and buildings. They can be thousands of years old or much more modern. Had the two heads that the Robson boys unearthed been mere Celtic heads, nothing much would have happened. Maybe they would have been taken to an expert to get validated. They might have ended up in a drawer in a museum somewhere, added to the tally of small stone craniums that the island is seeded with. It's what happened after the heads were dug up that made them infamous, transcending their status as mere possible Celtic heads to named and known cursed objects.

According to various newspaper accounts, the boys took the heads inside their house, and weird stuff started to happen immediately. Items flew across rooms of their own accord. The heads seemed to swivel on their neck stumps, their rough-cut eyes following the Robsons across the room. Poltergeist stuff, really. But the Robsons' neighbors, Nelly Dodd and her son Brian, got it far worse. They and the Robsons lived in semidetached housing, meaning they each lived in half of the same residential building and shared a wall. Over on the Dodd side, invisible entities pulled Brian's hair at night and, in what would become a defining part of the curse of the Hexham Heads, Nelly spotted a were-creature – in this case, a weresheep (part man, part sheep). It ran through the house on two legs and out the door and disappeared bleating into the night. That might sound silly now, but in the middle of the night it could be as terrifying as any classic movie monster.

This was quite the escalation for a couple of stone lumps tilled from the soil of a backyard. And word got out. The media picked up the story and circulated it far beyond the reach of local gossips, far enough even that things got academic – but in a weird way.

Dr. Anne Ross was a University of Edinburgh–educated scholar and archeologist focusing on Celtic traditions and artifacts. In addition to her academic work, she also had some less-than-academically-respectable fringe interests around paranormal phenomenon. So she was both the perfect person to investigate the stones and the worst person to investigate them. When she got her hands on the Hexham Heads, she estimated them to be Iron Age artifacts, some two millennia old.

She was so enamored with them that she ended up taking the heads to her house. Soon enough, she began detecting cold spots in her residence, a shadow presence, and doors opening and closing by themselves. Then it happened again. She was visited by a were-creature, this time a more

respectable werewolf, which acted just like the weresheep – running through her house until it vanished outside and into the night. She and her family eventually witnessed the creature multiple times in the house.

The testimony of an academic was the validation the Hexham Heads needed to really get their story to spread. And it was a unique situation: an academic who fanned flames around the incredible instead of wet-blanketing them. The wet blanket would eventually come, but from the testimony of a construction worker.

Desmond Craigie lived at 3 Rede Avenue before the Robsons. Once the infamy of the Hexham Heads reached him, he stepped forward and admitted to making the rough spheres in 1956. They were for his daughter, and he carved them during his lunch break at the concrete company he worked for. In fact, he made three. A chemical analysis was conducted with material removed from the heads, and it indicated that Craigie was telling the truth, even if he couldn't quite replicate the heads when he tried to do so to prove his point. It had been almost twenty years, after all – he hadn't honed his spooky head-carving craft.

Still, for many, the story ended there. The Hexham Heads had a mundane beginning in a residential garden, were completely misinterpreted by some superstitious Hexhamites and an overeager academic with a propensity for the nonscientific, and had their story spread around the country and world by gleeful media.

But plenty of cursed objects have mundane beginnings. There are two different cursed chairs in this book, for goodness' sake. But to think that a couple of stones with faces probably made as a lark somehow prompted a small invasion of were-creatures, or at least the perception of a small invasion of were-creatures? Sometimes we should just be thankful for the story.

To make matters even more interesting, the Hexham Heads eventually disappeared. The chain of provenance, along with Dr. Ross, included the University of Southampton, the Museum of Antiquities in Newcastle upon Tyne, and a few other researchers and paranormalists, but eventually the trail goes cold. All that remains are photographs and drawings of the two artifacts.

But we do know that whoever has them must have a high tolerance for were-creatures. And then there's the potential third Hexham Head that was never found. Maybe it's still in the dirt of 3 Rede Avenue, waiting to be reunited with the other two. And who knows what will happen then.

The Amber Room

PLACE OF ORIGIN:	INSTALLATIONS:
PRUSSIA	BERLIN CITY PALACE, PRUSSIA; WINTER PALACE, RUSSIA; CATHERINE PALACE, RUSSIA; KÖNIGSBERG CASTLE, GERMANY
ARTISTS:	**ESTIMATED VALUE:**
ANDRES SCHLÜTER, GOTTFRIED WOLFRAM	$500 MILLION
YEAR MADE:	**CURRENT LOCATION:**
1701	UNKNOWN

Most of us think of amber in a scientific context instead of an aesthetic one. Amber is the fossilized tree resin that traps and preserves bugs, lizards, and dinosaur feathers from prehistoric times. But it's pretty, like hardened honey, and is considered a semiprecious stone. It's one of the few organically created gemstones on the planet, along with pearls and ivory. But there is a much more pleasant way to get trapped in amber — by stepping inside one of the wonders of the twentieth century: the cursed Amber Room.

Built in 1701 in Prussia, the Amber Room was designed and built by sculptor Andres Schlüter and amber craftsman Gottfried Wolfram. It was a room fit for a palace and, in fact, was specially fitted for one — Charlottenburg Palace in Berlin, then the capital of the kingdom of Prussia. However, an executive decision was made somewhere along the line, and it ended up at Berlin City Palace instead.

Calling this thing a room is like calling the Burj Khalifa an office building. Many tons of exquisitely worked amber coated its walls, amber that was backed in gold leaf and encrusted with countless other semiprecious stones and reflecting mirrors. Standing inside of this amber-paneled room when it was lit was like being bathed in the glow of heaven.

Basically, it was worth showing off, which is what Berlin did when Russia's Peter the Great dropped by to say, "Hey, how's it going? Need help with your war?" Peter loved the room, and Friedrich II, King of Prussia, was so grateful for Peter's alliance against Sweden (which ended the Pomeranian War) that he gave it to him. In 1716, the walls were carefully dismantled, packed into eighteen boxes, and then re-erected at the Winter Palace in St. Petersburg.

In 1755, the room was moved again, this time by Czarina Elizabeth to Catherine Palace in the Russian town of Pushkin, where more amber was added and the room was enlarged until the total insurable value exceeded six tons of amber covering 590 square feet of paneling.

For almost two hundred years, the Amber Room was the golden heart of Catherine Palace. Then came the Nazis. On June 22, 1941, Adolf Hitler sent three million soldiers into the Soviet Union as part of Operation Barbarossa. The Amber Room was a specific target of that invasion; the Germans hoped to return the treasure to its country of origin.

The Russians tried to hide the room from the Nazi troops, at first by attempting to take the panels apart, but the ancient amber was brittle and their expertise not equal to the task.

Then they had a brilliant idea: they covered it in wallpaper.

But the Nazis knew shoddy interior design when they saw it and quickly uncovered the amber panels. They'd also brought their own amber experts, who took less than two days to take the room apart. It was then packed into twenty-seven boxes and rebuilt for Königsberg Castle. It stayed there until the end of the war when it and many of Germany's other looted treasures were evacuated in a panic.

And then, in 1944, the Amber Room disappeared. Nobody knows where it went. But there are theories. There are always theories. Some claimed to have seen it loaded aboard the transport ship *Wilhelm Gustloff* . . . right before a Russian submarine torpedoed the ship in the Baltic Sea, killing as many as 9,400 people. If that's true, those brilliants panels are finally darkened, submerged far from any source of light.

Some say it was packed onto a train and sent off to a secret underground bunker outside of Dresden. Others point to the final destination being a lagoon in Lithuania or a silver mine on the border of Germany and Czechia.

Some believe that the Amber Room never made it out of Königsberg Castle, which was bombed into ruins by the Soviets. Those ruins were pulled down in 1968 and the central square of Kaliningrad was built atop the site.

Small pieces have surfaced since 1944, seeming to lend credence to the idea that the room was successfully packed up for evacuation. But, in the end, nobody knows what happened to those twenty-seven boxes full of solid sunlight. Although many think it's cursed.

The curse starts with a man named Alfred Rohde, who is pointed to as the first victim. He was in charge of the Königsberg Castle museum and also in charge of getting the Amber Room out of the museum. He stuck around after the Germans evacuated and the Soviets had taken over. Many think he was the only one who knew where the Amber Room was stashed. As a result, he was interrogated on multiple occasions by the KGB. However, one day he didn't show up for a follow-up questioning session, and the KGB were informed that he, along with his wife, had died suddenly the previous night from typhus. When the KGB investigated, they couldn't find the bodies, nor the doctor who had pronounced them dead.

The next victim of the curse is General Yuri Gusev, a Russian intelligence officer. Apparently, the local media had been writing a lot about the Amber Room and the efforts to find it, and at some point it was determined that Gusev had been leaking information to them. Not long after, he died in a car crash.

Another victim of the curse is Georg Stein. He was a German soldier and treasure hunter who was on the trail of the Amber Room in a forest in Bavaria. In 1987, he was found dead in that forest, his naked body split open with a scalpel.

All of these deaths are mysterious, but not necessarily in a supernatural way. But that doesn't mean there's no curse attached to the Amber Room. It just might be that "curse" here is a metaphor. In 2004, a *Forbes* magazine reporter interviewed Dr. Ivan Sautov, then director of the Catherine Palace Museum, who, when questioned about the deaths connected to the Amber Room, said, "The people who have concealed the Amber Room may be members of a closed circle, and anyone who comes too close to this circle will die."

Maybe the Amber Room isn't meant to be found. Maybe it's tired of moving around. Of being gawked at. Of being compared to heaven. It's a room made of prehistoric tree blood. Maybe it's ready to be extinct.

And Russia seems to agree, as it gave up the search for the Amber Room, forging forward to build a brand-new one instead. The new Amber Room project started in 1979 and took eleven million dollars and twenty-five years to complete. But in 2004, Catherine Palace finally got its golden heart back. It remains to be seen if the curse applies to replicas.

The Treasure of Cahuenga Pass

PLACE OF ORIGIN:	VICTIMS CLAIMED:
MEXICO	NINE
YEAR ASSEMBLED:	**CURRENT LOCATION:**
1864	UNKNOWN
ORIGINAL VALUE:	
$200,000	

The New Testament tells us that the love of money is the root of all evil. The Notorious B.I.G. phrased it as "Mo money, mo problems." You could say that every dollar in your mobile wallet is a cursed object, and you would not be far from the truth. But the Treasure of Cahuenga Pass has an actual body count.

The origin of the full tale seems to be the posthumously published memoirs of a prominent Angeleno named Horace Bell, who died in 1918 after a life of gold mining and ranching and lawyering and authoring books about the Wild West. He claimed to have stitched together the story of the Treasure of Cahuenga Pass himself based on three different sources: a soldier named Captain Henry Malcolm, a tavern keeper named Etchepare, and a policeman named Jose Correa.

This story starts in Mexico in 1864 after a civil war that found Benito Juárez, a Mexican of Zapotec origin, as the last president standing. Napoleon III of France, looking to get a foothold in America and backed by the Catholic Church – which wanted a theocracy in Mexico – sent Maximilian, Archduke of Austria, to Mexico to take over as emperor. Juárez fled from the European army Maximilian brought with him, but he immediately launched plans to take back the government from the invaders.

He had a nightmare that if he took the treasure to Los Angeles, he would die.

Juárez collected donations from Mexican patriots to fund the cause, creating a war chest of more than $200,000, an astronomical sum in today's dollars. Four men took this box of gold and diamonds and pearls and cash to San Francisco to buy guns. One died en route. He was the first victim of the as-yet-unnamed Treasure of Cahuenga Pass.

The other three made it to San Francisco, only to find its vertiginous hills crawling with the French. They detoured to the wilderness outside the city, divided the treasure into six parcels, wrapped each in buckskin, and buried them in separate holes. When it was safe, the three men returned to retrieve the treasure and finish their mission, only to find all six buckskin parcels missing. They fought among themselves, and two of them were killed as a result. That's three bodies. The fourth was jailed, but eventually exonerated of murder. But then he was gunned down in Tombstone, Arizona. Four bodies.

Later it was discovered that a local shepherd named Diego Moreno had witnessed the three men burying the treasure, and then snuck down and taken it for himself after they left. And here's where we get to the Cahuenga Pass. Suddenly rich, Moreno ditched his life of lonely sheep vigils and headed south to Los Angeles. On his way, he went through the Cahuenga Pass, a rugged wagon trail that passed through the lowest part of the Santa Monica Mountains. *Cahuenga* is a Native American word for "place of little hills."

At this point, Moreno stopped at a small tavern for the night. While there, he had a nightmare that if he took the treasure to Los Angeles, he would die. So he didn't. He buried the parcels of treasure at the southern end of the pass to figure out what to do with them later and continued to the City of Angels un-treasured. He died there anyway of an unidentified illness, in the arms of his friend, Jesus Martinez. Before Moreno became body number five, though, he told Martinez where the treasure was buried.

Martinez and his stepson, Jose Correa, trucked out to dig up the treasure. Shovels in hand, Martinez suffered a seizure and died. That's six bodies. Correa panicked and fled from what was obviously a cursed treasure, saving himself from becoming body number seven.

And so the treasure sat untouched for two decades, until 1885 when another shepherd stumbled across one of the parcels. Overjoyed at his fortune and, like Moreno before him, tired of staring at sheep, he took that parcel and boarded a boat to Spain to start a new life. Upon arrival, he stumbled and fell into the sea, with the treasure that he had sewn into his clothes to protect it now dragging him to the bottom. He drowned, becoming body number seven.

About a decade later, his stepfather's death a dim, confusing memory, Correa made plans to return to the site of the treasure and finish what he and Martinez had started so long ago. But before he could leave, the man who avoided becoming body number seven was shot by his brother-in-law and became body number eight.

Then came the twentieth century. Cahuenga Pass was paved over, becoming the main highway between Los Angeles and the San Fernando Valley. By this time, the Treasure of the Cahuenga Pass had become legendary. It had even been turned into a CBS radio drama. In November 1939, a team composed of a mining expert named Henry Jones, a mechanic named Walter Combes, and his uncle, an inventor named Ennis Combes, took a newfangled metal detector made by Ennis to search out the hoard, which they believed to be under the parking lot of the Hollywood Bowl. It was a big deal. The media followed the treasure hunters' every step. The public came out to watch. The local supervisory board gave them permission to dig, as long as they received a cut.

The team pinpointed what they thought was an extremely likely spot for the treasure, fourteen feet below the asphalt. Everyone got excited – except for the Combeses. For some reason – maybe the curse, maybe all the scrutiny around their device and findings – the uncle and nephew got cold feet on that hot California tarmac and left, taking their metal detector with them.

Undaunted, Henry Jones assembled another team, including Hollywood stuntman Ray Johnson and another inventor with a metal detector, Frank Hoekstra. And they dug: in the not-as-grueling but still quite grueling November sun, amidst all the onlookers and interviewers and photographers and amateur treasure hunters. They dug for twenty-four days, displacing some one hundred tons of earth. Their handiwork was a nine-foot-wide, forty-two-foot deep hole in the Cahuenga Pass. An empty, nine-foot-wide, forty-two-feet-deep hole. They would have kept digging, but they hit a giant boulder and finally realized that the mission was a failure.

A month later, Jones committed suicide by car exhaust. His suicide note attributed it to his recent divorce. Regardless, in the lore he became body number nine — and, so far, the last victim of the cursed treasure of Cahuenga Pass.

And that might be thanks to the supervisory board denying all treasure-hunting requests after that, except for a one-day hunt by a man named William W. Boyle, who tried to find it with a dowsing rod. Lucky for him, he came up empty-handed. Today, the cursed Treasure of the Cahuenga Pass is still missing, presumably buried under asphalt and crushing Los Angeles traffic.

All told, the treasure took down nine people and thwarted a major modern treasure hunt. Oh, and remember Maximillian, whose usurpation as the emperor of Mexico kickstarted this whole curse? He was executed soon after his ascension to the throne, and his wife went insane as a result. Curse or not, the more money we come across, the more problems we see.

The Business of Cursed Objects

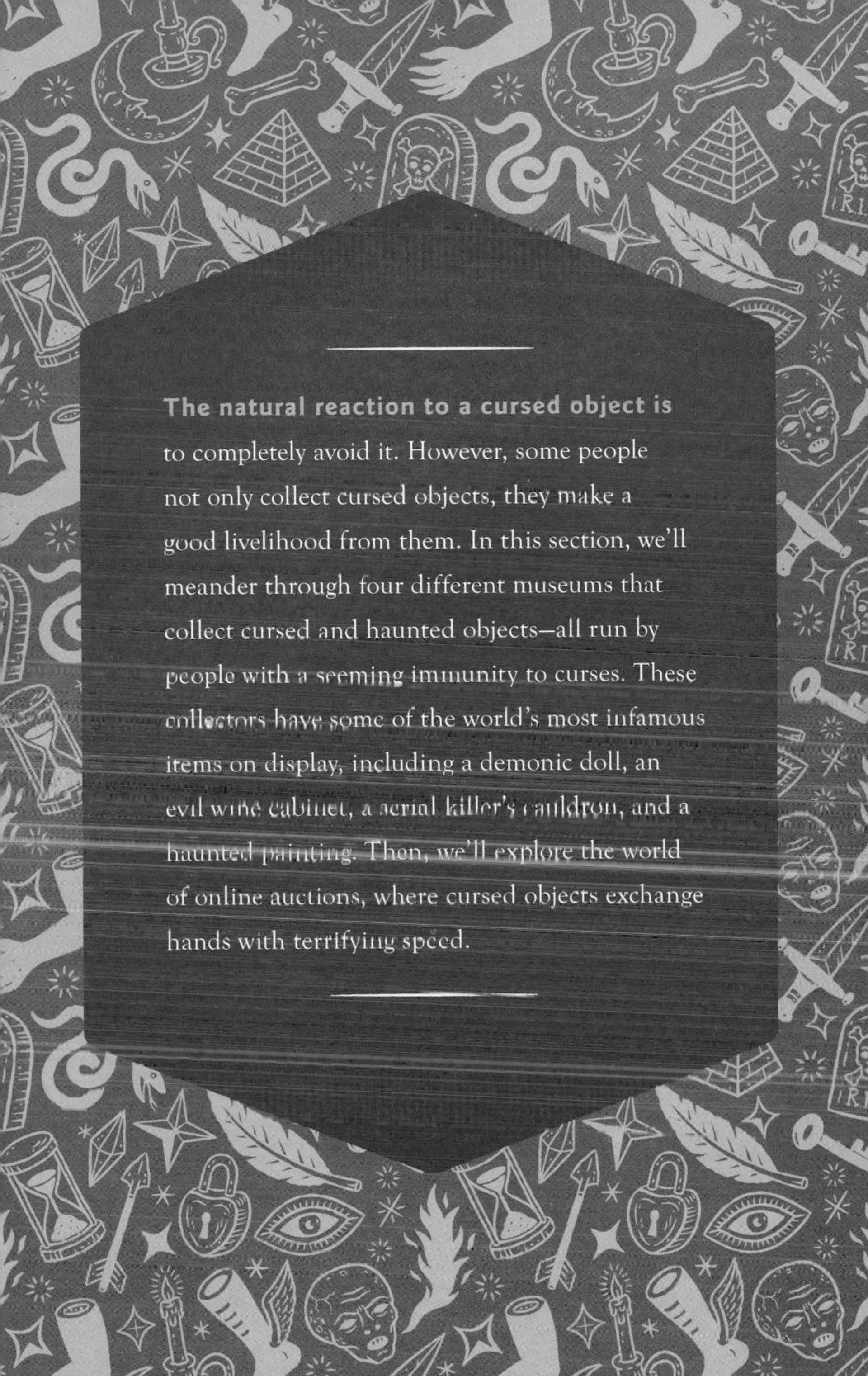

The natural reaction to a cursed object is to completely avoid it. However, some people not only collect cursed objects, they make a good livelihood from them. In this section, we'll meander through four different museums that collect cursed and haunted objects—all run by people with a seeming immunity to curses. These collectors have some of the world's most infamous items on display, including a demonic doll, an evil wine cabinet, a serial killer's cauldron, and a haunted painting. Then, we'll explore the world of online auctions, where cursed objects exchange hands with terrifying speed.

WARNING
POSITIVELY
DO NOT OPEN

Annabelle the Doll and the Warren Collection

PLACE OF ORIGIN:	NOTABLE OWNERS:
CONNECTICUT	ED AND LORRAINE WARREN
YEAR ACQUIRED:	**CURRENT LOCATION:**
1968	WARREN'S OCCULT MUSEUM, CONNECTICUT

Raggedy Ann was a twentieth-century pop culture phenomenon. She was a simple doll with red yarn hair and a triangle nose and a brother named Raggedy Andy. Invented by children's book author Johnny Gruelle, Raggedy Ann had millions of books in print, toys and merchandise, animated movies, and a TV series. Then she became the most infamous haunted doll of all time — all thanks to a husband-and-wife paranormal investigation team who taught pop culture how to chase ghosts and demons.

Let's start with Ed and Lorraine Warren. So many spooky things start with Ed and Lorraine Warren. Ed Warren's bio calls him a "self-taught demonologist," and his wife Lorraine was a professed clairvoyant and medium. They met each other as teens in the early 1940s in Bridgeport, Connecticut, married a year or so later, and then set out on an adventure that would define the modern paranormal landscape in the popular imagination while creating a ghostbusting media empire that including novelizations, movies, and talk show appearances. So big was that empire that most of their cases are known by the titles of the movies they spawned: *The Amityville Horror* (1979), *The Demon Murder Case* (1983), *The Haunted* (1991), *The Haunting in Connecticut* (2009), *The Conjuring* (2013), and many more. Ghost, demons, werewolves, Bigfoot – these lovebirds took them all on, especially when the licensing rights seemed lucrative. They claimed to have investigated some 10,000 cases of paranormal activity in their career.

In 1952, they started the New England Society for Psychic Research from their home in Monroe, Connecticut. Over the years, all the cursed and haunted and possessed objects amassed from their adventures grew into the Warren's Occult Museum, operating out of that same house in Monroe and open to the public for events and by invitation. In the early 1970s, they added Annabelle to that collection.

Annabelle was one of the tens of thousands of Raggedy Ann dolls given to children as birthday and Christmas presents over the years. This one, however, was cursed. Or, technically, possessed. Or, more technically, attached to an inhuman demonic spirit. But so popular is the story of Annabelle that she needs to be included in this book, cursed object or not.

According to the Warrens, the doll was given as a present to a nursing student named Donna by her mother in 1970. Soon after Donna received the doll, it started moving around her apartment, seemingly on its own. Donna would come home to find it in a different position than where she had left it — sometimes in a completely different place in the room. Donna had a roommate named Angie and a friend named Lou who was staying there at the time, but they professed ignorance of the doll's antics.

Soon that simple game of Where's Raggedy Ann Now? escalated to notes left around the apartment in what looked like a child's handwriting. The messages were simple but startling: "Help us." "Help Lou." Lou had no idea why he was being singled out.

Donna was able to ignore the moving doll and the strange messages, but when the doll began to bleed, she called in a medium. The medium determined that the doll was inhabited by a girl named Annabelle Higgins, who had been murdered and left in the lot where Donna's apartment building now stood.

The messages were simple but startling: "Help us." "Help Lou."

Donna held on to the doll, taking pity on the child's spirit inside. But then Raggedy Ann, or Annabelle, got vicious. One night, Lou awoke to find the doll clambering up his body and trying to strangle him. Its little floppy arms felt like iron bars, and he was paralyzed. He blacked out, but fortunately awoke the next morning.

The next time Lou was attacked by the doll, an invisible claw slashed his chest, ripping his shirt and drawing blood. This convinced the roommates that what was inside that doll was no mere child victim. So they called a priest named Hegan, who called a priest named Cooke, who called the Warrens.

Ed and Lorraine diagnosed the doll as demonic and took it home, where they encountered some trouble themselves, including the car they drove it home in veering and stalling throughout the trip and the doll levitating and attacking clergy at the house.

They eventually stuck Annabelle in a glass case in their museum with a sign stating: "Warning: Positively Do Not Open." But its most dangerous attack was still to come, at least according to the Warrens' website. It tells a vague story of one museum visitor who, after making fun of Annabelle, died in a motorcycle accident on their way home.

And, of course, like many of the Warren cases, Annabelle got a movie. Three, as of this writing, in fact: *Annabelle* in 2014, *Annabelle: Creation* in 2017, and *Annabelle Comes Home* in 2019. Plus a cameo in *The Conjuring*. In these movies, she wasn't played by the goofy, beloved Raggedy Ann icon, but rather by a large antique Victorian doll that seems more in line with her creepy reputation and a better face for a horror franchise.

And while Annabelle is the most famous item in the Warren's Occult Museum, she's not the only cursed object. For instance, there's the Doll of Shadows, a five-foot-tall horror made of feathers, bone, and fabric created to curse enemies. Take a photo of it and write your enemy's name on the back, and the creature will appear in that person's dreams and stop their heart. It doesn't have its own movie. Not yet, anyway.

All the documentation and testimony for Annabelle and the other objects in the Warren's Occult Museum comes from the Warrens themselves. And the other side of their story – the one not revealed in the *Conjuring* movie series that portrays them as sensitive, thoughtful, unlikely forces against evil – is that they were regularly accused throughout their career as being spotlight-chasing frauds, liars, and con artists preying on emotionally disturbed people. But in the paranormal world, that's as minor a speedbump as sex scandals in politics.

Ed died in 2006, days before his eightieth birthday. Lorraine died in 2019 at the age of ninety-three, days before I wrote this entry. The eventual destiny of the Warren's Occult Museum – and Annabelle in particular – is at the present time disconcertingly unknown.

John Zaffis Museum of the Paranormal

John Zaffis has been chasing the paranormal since he saw an apparition of his grandfather at the foot of his bed when he was a teenager in the early 1970s. From there, he had a relatively direct path into the field. His aunt and uncle were Ed and Lorraine Warren, the famous team who investigated thousands of paranormal incidents, including the Amityville Horror, Snedeker Haunting, and Enfield Poltergeist cases. He even worked with them on some of those investigations.

Over the decades, Zaffis developed his own brand in the field, writing books and giving talks and making media appearances. At some point, he began to specialize in cursed and haunted objects, so much so that from 2011 to 2013 he starred in his own paranormal reality show on the SyFy channel called *Haunted Collector*, in which he acted as a sort of paranormal junk removal service, taking everything from cursed and haunted guns and jewelry to cursed and haunted

medical instruments and (of course) dolls out of the houses of people who had been experiencing bad luck and creepy phenomena because of those objects.

Long before his TV show, though, Zaffis's affinity for cursed and haunted objects incarnated itself into a collection full of items from his investigations and oddities sent directly to him by people who had heard about him, always accompanied by a "Here, you take it!" type letter. The collection grew large enough that it had to be housed in a separate building behind his home in Stratford, Connecticut. The John Zaffis Museum of the Paranormal opened officially sometime in the early 2000s, although it's a private museum that can be visited only by invitation. I once received that invitation.

Walking into the single large room that holds most of the objects feels like meandering into a flea market or an antique shop. It's a jumble of objects of no immediately discernable order. And, after long consideration, they remain of no discernable order. There are shelves and piles full of masks and jewelry and clothing and paintings and statuettes and dishware and, of course, dolls (so, so many dolls). The dolls range from antique marionettes to clowns (so, so many clowns) to a Winnie-the-Pooh dressed like Santa Claus, the latter of which is one of the few pieces in the collection imprisoned in a glass case. On my visit, no objects were levitating or talking or glowing or otherwise indicating that this messy array was anything but a random basement collection ready for an estate sale. None of the items were marked with informational placards. Zaffis keeps all the stories in his head.

One such story involves a doll he calls the Joker. Wearing a pointed red hat and frilly gold shirt, it looks like a jester figure of the sort someone might collect, as opposed to a child's toy. It was a gift from one woman to her friend. A Christmas gift, in fact. But no sooner did the recipient unwrap the gift than strange things started to occur in her house, driving her crazy. Somehow she quickly connected it all back to the Joker, called up her friend, and called her out on it. The woman admitted that she put a curse on the doll. Apparently, she was in love with the friend's husband and was hoping this cursed doll would become a wedge in the relationship that she could take advantage of.

Another cursed object in the collection was a blue, old-fashioned-looking military jacket. Apparently it was purchased at an estate sale by a teenage girl with an interest in military regalia. When the girl wore it, she got cold, and later she started to have strange nightmares about soldiers. The nightmares disturbed her, and the girl contacted Zaffis to get his opinion. His opinion was, quite sensibly, to stop wearing the garment. She agreed with him, but could not stop wearing it, like she was compelled to don the strange coat. So Zaffis took it back to his place and stuck it on a dress mannequin in a corner by a velvet painting of a clown (so, so many clowns).

Other items included a sword used in occult rituals that called up dark figures, an old school desk that moved on its own, a dark idol with red eyes used in black magic rituals, and, maybe my favorite, an Easter decoration with a curse on it that a Muslim man had given to a Jewish woman.

Whether these objects are technically cursed or technically haunted isn't a line Zaffis draws often, although he seems to prefer the term *haunted*. Admittedly, it's a much more marketable designation. Zaffis usually describes what the objects are in terms of the "energy" connected to them. Sometimes it's the intelligent energy of a spirit, other times it's unmotivated negative energy. On his website, he describes the pieces this way: "Although the items are not 'possessed,' energy can be sent towards an object. Items can hold energy within or around them, and it is usually the result of the energy being sent to the object by an individual."

If keeping one cursed object in your house is a bad call,

then keeping hundreds must surely be paranormal masochism. However, according to Zaffis, each acquisition undergoes a binding ritual before being added to his collection. He describes that binding ritual in his delightfully titled 2014 book, *Haunted by the Things You Love*, cowritten with Rosemary Ellen Guiley. The main ingredients are sunlight, sea salt, holy water, prayer, and sometimes crystals, all of which combine to cleanse and infuse the object with positive energy.

But why keep the cursed objects at all? Even after all that sanctification and pasteurization and sanitization? According to Zaffis, attempting to destroy cursed and haunted objects or throwing them out can cause even more trouble, so he believes his home for wayward cursed objects is actually the safest form of disposal. Although he has been known to bury the more recalcitrant objects underground or drop them into deep bodies of water.

Besides, if he destroyed them, he wouldn't be the Haunted Collector.

Blessed Objects

The universe likes balance, and so it makes sense that if an object can be cursed, it can also be blessed.

There are two types of blessed objects. The first is literal blessed objects, items that have been prayed over by a member of a clergy. They appear often in the Catholic religion and include crucifixes, saint medallions, communion chalices, and holy relics. However, every religion or spiritual belief system has some version of this concept, as well. Whatever the source, these blessed objects are meant to protect their owners from evil, even the evil of a cursed object.

The other type of blessed objects is good luck charms or lucky charms. Unlike literal blessed objects, no action has been performed upon them to make them lucky. They either are such inherently because of what the object is (for instance, rabbit feet, horseshoes, four-leaf clovers, mojo bags, scarab beetles, crickets — there are actually quite a lot) or because of our personal experience with the item. Maybe it's a lucky penny because you found it on the sidewalk on the same day that you got a promotion at work. Or a lucky jacket because you were wearing it when you met your significant other.

Obviously, the biggest problem with discussing blessed objects and lucky charms is that . . . they're boring. Or at least not as interesting as cursed objects. The story of the Hope Diamond is just far more fascinating than the story of the Pope's diadem.

Zak Bagans's The Haunted Museum

This building is known to contain ghosts/spirits and cursed objects. By entering you agree that management will not be liable for any actions by unseen forces.

That's the sign that greeted me in the Haunted Museum's lobby, which was full of dolls and electric candles and antique Halloween decorations. It smelled of incense. The statement on the sign was close to the language on the waiver I had to initial before I entered, and also to the language our tour guide made us repeat while raising our hands before she would take us through the old mansion owned by Zak Bagans.

Zak Bagans is the star of the paranormal reality show *Ghost Adventures*. It debuted in 2008 on the Travel Channel and, as of this writing, is still going strong nineteen seasons later, making Bagans a rich man. And what did he do with all that money? He bought a historic house in Las Vegas, turned it into a museum, and stuffed it full of all the spookiest stuff money could buy.

The Haunted Museum opened in October 2017. Visitors can only witness the dim, atmospherically decorated museum as part of a guided tour. And that tour reveals the attraction to be more a museum of the macabre than of the paranormal, featuring jaw-dropping (and stomach-heaving) items – Charles Manson's ashes, Ted Bundy's glasses, pill bottles owned by Truman Capote, a chair from the bedroom where Michael Jackson died, and Sharon Tate's wedding dress. A severed head is on display in a U-shaped room that allows everyone in the tour group to have one-on-one time with it. Jack Kevorkian's van/mobile suicide clinic takes up a large room inside the house. Bagans displays serial killer Robert Berdella's blood- and feces-stained torture bed beside blowups of the photos Berdella took of his victims. And there are lots of cursed objects. Which sometimes seem tame by comparison.

One room decorated to look like an old barn (complete with creaky floorboards) is dedicated to a black cauldron owned by notorious death fetishist and murderer Ed Gein. It is assumed that he used the large pot for grisly purposes because, well, it's Ed Gein. He made masks and clothing and furniture out of human skin and bones. A sign above it reads: "Ed Gein's Cursed Cauldron." The tour guide regaled us with a story of some half a dozen people connected to the cauldron who had died.

A cursed human skull (distinct from a set of thirteen human skulls we saw in another room) shares a library with a cursed doll like some inanimate version of *The Odd Couple*. The skull was found during an investigation of an old mining hotel. Bagans took the skull home, and, he says, it unleashed a presence that eventually chased him from the house. The doll – which wears a long, trailing white dress with stains on it and is labeled "Murder Doll" – was ostensibly donated by a family whose great-great-grandfather was murdered by his son after the former tried to kill the family with a shotgun. It happened in front of the man's daughter, who was carrying the doll and was close enough for the blood spatter to hit them both.

There's also the infamous dybbuk box to which I dedicated an entire chapter earlier in this book (see page 103), but such is the glut of the macabre in the museum that not every piece gets equally high billing. For instance, shoved on a shelf with a hundred other items like so much bric-a-brac is a cursed Nazi helmet, the lining of which still bears skull and hair fragments from the wearer's violent death.

In one room is the largest concentration of cursed items this side of King Tut's tomb. The cursed mirror of Bela Lugosi, the actor who portrayed Dracula in the 1931 Universal Studios movie of the same name, hangs on a wall. It is supposed to have been used for occult purposes and then later witnessed a man's murder by the mob. It stayed covered under a dark curtain until we were told to line up to peer into its depths one at a time. There is an original *Crying Boy* painting (and a facsimile beside it), also discussed in this book (see page 94), and a tall painting from the 2006 movie *Silent Hill*, whose previous owner's entire collection of oddity burned to the ground after he delivered the piece to Bagans.

There is also a painting by Bill Stoneham, who painted the infamous *The Hands Resist Him* in 1972. That creepy rendering, which predates the work in Bagans's collection, shows a boy and a large girl doll in front of a dark glass door behind which can be seen about a dozen hands. After being bought at an exhibition, it was found decades later in an abandoned building and listed on eBay in February 2000, with a spooky summary from its owner that accused the painting's subjects of moving around and even exiting into the real world. It became Internet-famous, was dubbed the "eBay Haunted Painting," and was bought for more than a thousand dollars. Bagans couldn't get his hands on that original work, so he commissioned Stoneham to paint a prequel for it, called *The Hands Invent Him.*

The Haunted Museum experience is an intense one. One person on my tour dropped out with a headache and the sweats after spending time in a room with a haunted doll (and a strobe light and an extremely loud spirit box). Others opted to not enter rooms, waiting outside for the tour to continue. Which begs the question: "Why have so many disturbing and (if the multiple waivers are to be believed) dangerous items in one place and open to the public?" The answer given by the museum is the usual one: to educate about the paranormal world and to keep the objects from doing damage in open circulation. You could even say zoos are analogous, being full of deadly animals but nevertheless open to touring school groups.

Perhaps the truest answer can be found in the final thing our tour guide said as she gestured toward a door: "Last is the scariest room in the house . . . the gift shop."

The Traveling Museum of the Paranormal and Occult

Greg Newkirk was a teenager in Pennsylvania breaking into abandoned houses with friends, looking for ghosts but finding meth labs. Dana Matthews was on the cast of an early-millennium paranormal reality show in Canada called *The Girly Ghosthunters*. The two met via their rival ghost hunting websites. They eventually married and opened the Traveling Museum of the Paranormal and Occult. You know, the typical boy-meets-girl story.

But first they had to get fired from their day jobs. The Newkirks both worked at a travel startup in Cincinnati creating web content. When their department got the axe, they decided to create their own income stream, one more in line with their paired passion for the paranormal. They wanted the ghosts to pay for the groceries. They amassed a small collection of haunted and cursed objects and started touring paranormal conventions with it. They called it the Traveling Museum of the Paranormal and Occult. The museum grew as people sent them items that they wanted – or needed – out of their homes and lives. The Newkirks opened a Patreon to fund the museum and then became successful enough that they now spend their days as what they call "professional weirdos."

They're weird even among the already-weird paranormal community. For instance, they posit that the reason that no physical proof of Bigfoot has yet been found is that these creatures aren't physical. "Bigfoot is a ghost," is how they semi-jokingly refer to it. In the docu-series *Hellier* that they produced and starred in, they chase down cave goblins in Kentucky after an anonymous tip and, after finding less than nothing, turn that non-discovery into a revelation around the synchronicity of small things . . . a noise in the woods, a tin can in a cave, a reference in an old paranormal book, all combining into some sort of message to them from beyond. It's like the opposite of Occam's razor. When the weird doesn't pan out, go weirder.

They have similarly unconventional ideas about the cursed and haunted objects in their museum. The Newkirks treat the objects almost like roommates and sometimes even friends. They keep them displayed in the living space of their Covington, Kentucky home. They give offerings to them, talk to them, and make sure they're comfortable during the trips to paranormal conventions, where the Newkirks give talks and let people interact with these objects. They believe people shouldn't pick fights with the paranormal or trap paranormal items in glass cases or treat them like horror movie props. They think people should be more open with the objects, that they should engage with these objects on their own terms and with curiosity.

And maybe that hopefulness and sentimentality is the reason that none of the objects in their collection have achieved the level of infamy as, say, the Warrens' Annabelle doll (page 173) or Zak Bagans's dybbuk box (page 103). But they have some interesting artifacts.

The object that has become a mascot for the museum is a two-foot-tall dark wooden figure called the Idol of Nightmares – nicknamed Billy. Billy the Idol. According to the Newkirks, it was found in a burlap sack under a home in Dayton, Ohio, and was donated to them because of the nightmares it caused the people who lived there. And, apparently, kept causing. Since joining the museum, Billy the Idol has had this signature effect on whoever comes into contact with it. And that includes Greg, who claims that his nightmares include obscure instructions for building equipment to talk to the dead. The Newkirks believe the idol comes from the Congo and was used by a holy man as a "paranormal telephone" to communicate with some mysterious entity.

They also claim that the idol might have saved their lives. On their way back from a paranormal convention in 2016, the two received a tip about a red-eyed monster that haunted a cemetery in rural Friendsville, Maryland. It was late at night, and they decided to check it out. While looking for the cemetery, they were rear-ended by a car full of people. One of those people, a man in a bolo tie with an eye full of blood and a bruise that covered the entire side of his face, exited the car and insisted they exchange insurance information, even though Greg didn't think the damage was enough to worry about. As Greg got back in his car to grab his insurance card, one of the boxes in the back – they think the one that held Billy – started vibrating and knocking around so loudly that Greg turned to see what was happening. What he saw was the bruised man opening his trunk and two men getting out of the back seat of the other car. Greg floored the gas pedal until the entire state was in the rearview. The Newkirks believe that if the idol hadn't reacted, they might have been robbed and killed.

Another object of theirs that hasn't turned as friendly is the Dark Mirror. It's a small sheet of black glass in an 8-by-10 frame and was used for scrying — a practice similar to crystal ball gazing. They received it from a woman who said her mother had bought it to scry with and then became obsessed with it, to the point that her personality started changing. Eventually, she admitted it was evil and hid it under a black shroud in her closet. She let her daughter donate it to the Newkirks' museum.

The first time the Newkirks put the mirror on public display, a woman looked into it and claimed to see her own decaying corpse. So did another. Others felt negative vibes when they peered into its shiny black surface. At other events, people experienced their faces warping or their reflection moving or dark blobs hovering near them.

Back at home, the Newkirks kept the Dark Mirror covered in the black shroud on their mantel. Then the mirror started uncovering itself every night. They put a motion-activated trail cam (normally used for hunting Bigfoot's ghost) on it, but the memory card was empty of images every morning. Eventually, other objects began acting up, leading them to believe that the glass pane sucks up and stores energy like a battery, which in turn affects the other objects. They decided to store it away. No more mantel spot beside their wedding photos.

The Traveling Museum of the Paranormal and Occult has plenty more strange objects with strange stories. There never seems to be an abatement in people sending the Newkirks items. Like a Ouija board made from the floorboards at a murder scene, a painting that flings itself from the wall, and, yes, plenty of dolls. If you want to hold a nightmare-producing idol or peer into an evil black mirror yourself, look out for them. They are probably coming to a town near you, with a trunk full of cursed and haunted objects.

Cursed on eBay

You don't have to dig through dark castle attics or the baked soil of long-disappeared civilizations to find cursed objects for yourself. You just have to grab your phone and go to eBay. At any given time, scores of cursed objects are for sale on the online auction site – dolls, stones, jewelry, statuettes, the ashes of demons – it's all on there.

I would know. I bought a cursed object off eBay when I started writing this book. In fact, some of the more infamous modern cursed objects have ended up on eBay at some point. Like the dybbuk box (see page 103) and Bill Stoneham's 1972 painting *The Hands Resist Him* (see page 186).

My cursed object wasn't so Internet-famous as these – or so expensive. But facing a year-long immersion into the world of cursed objects, I decided I needed to buy one. And eBay seemed a much safer bet than heisting the Hope Diamond or re-defiling Tut's tomb. So I typed "cursed objects" into the search bar and found countless wonders.

I found a cursed wooden African mask (circa 1988) that came from the home of an "ex Satanist and Chaos magician" and had been adjacent to various dark rituals and acts of violence. I found a cursed wooden bowl stand from the apartment of evicted Satanists that caused people to see shadow people, feel phantom touches, and hear voices. It could also hold a bowl pretty well. A cursed pocket watch that held the "demon spirit of a moldavian [*sic*] evil nurse." A cursed Buddha head that made items disappear and cats fall over. A small, cursed wooden box owned by the seller's grandfather, who had killed himself. It contained two chess pieces that switched places in the box when you weren't looking. (The starting bid was $1,000, or $49 installments for 24 months.) A cursed dybbuk ring. A cursed dybbuk broach. And dolls. So, so many dolls.

I chose my cursed object carefully. Turns out, many of them have reserves in the three figures. I wasn't about to invest that much into what was basically a book gimmick. In fact, I spent so much time trying to find the perfect cursed object that eBay started running targeted ads for cursed objects across my online experience: "Cursed Items on eBay: Seriously We Have Cursed Items" was one headline.

Eventually, I found the perfect object. It was the right size, the right type, the right cost. It was a bronze bulldog about three and a half inches long and two inches tall, and its opening price was only $11 (plus $3.78 shipping). The seller was from North Carolina. She had a strong positive feedback rating, but it was her eBay summary that really won me over:

Cursed Object
Evil, Beware. Brass or Bronze Bulldog

My father, who collected dog figurines, purchased this when he was a boy in the 1930's from a Chinese business . . . the owner of the business did not want to sell it, but my dad persisted and the man sold it with the warning that he would curse it . . . he

> mumbled a curse as my dad left with the dog . . . our family has been burdened all my life, unable to get ahead financially, illness, family strife . . . I need to rid our life of this horrid curse . . . please let me end this . . . purchase it, give it to your worst enemy, your ex husband, or anyone else you want to inflict bad luck and sadness on . . . Absolutely no refunds or returns on this object . . . I do not want this in my presence any more.
>
> I am starting this at $11.00 because 11 is my lucky number . . . hoping this will begin a new phase in my family's life.

I ended up being the only bidder. When I won, I received an email letting me know that the cursed object would be on its way as soon as the seller cleansed her house and officially passed the curse on to mine. I awaited the tracking number.

She really knew what I was looking to hear, and it made me think that perhaps that's what she was actually selling: an experience. That idea was further supported when I received the box a mere four days later (I can see why she had such a good rating on eBay). It was an ordinary USPS Priority Mail small flat-rate box. On its white cardboard flanks, she had written more warnings to me in pink ink: "May you live in interesting times. May you attract the attention of people in power. May you get what you ask for." That last sentence was underlined.

When I pulled the eagerly awaited cursed object out of the box, it was heavy for its size, making me think it might be a paperweight. I scrutinized the dull metal but could find no identifying marks anywhere on the pooch, which helped the story a good bit. The last thing I wanted to see punched into its belly was "Made in China" or "© 2019."

I received the item in early March, and I set it on a shelf in my office. For the next two months, while I worked on this book, the cursed dog stared at me from its perch, and every once in a while, I would pause after writing a sentence about a victim of a cursed object and stare back. But by the end of April, nothing bad had happened to me.

I decided to up the stakes. I took it on vacation with me. I stuck it in my backpack, and my family flew down to St. Augustine, Florida, for a week (which, yes, maybe was slightly inconsiderate to the rest of the people on that plane). I didn't tell my wife about the stunt until we were relaxed and sunburnt a few days in. "I could have gone the whole vacation without knowing that," she said. But the vacation was a great one.

Overall, and somewhat disappointingly, it was a really great year for me in numerous ways. And, while having a souvenir of my time visiting and researching cursed objects is well worth the eleven dollars plus shipping, part of me wished that it would have introduced enough weird chaos into my life that I would have been forced to send it to John Zaffis, Zak Bagans, or the Newkirks. But who knows? Like every dog, maybe this one's still getting used to its new home before its personality really starts to assert itself.

Why Aren't These Objects Cursed?

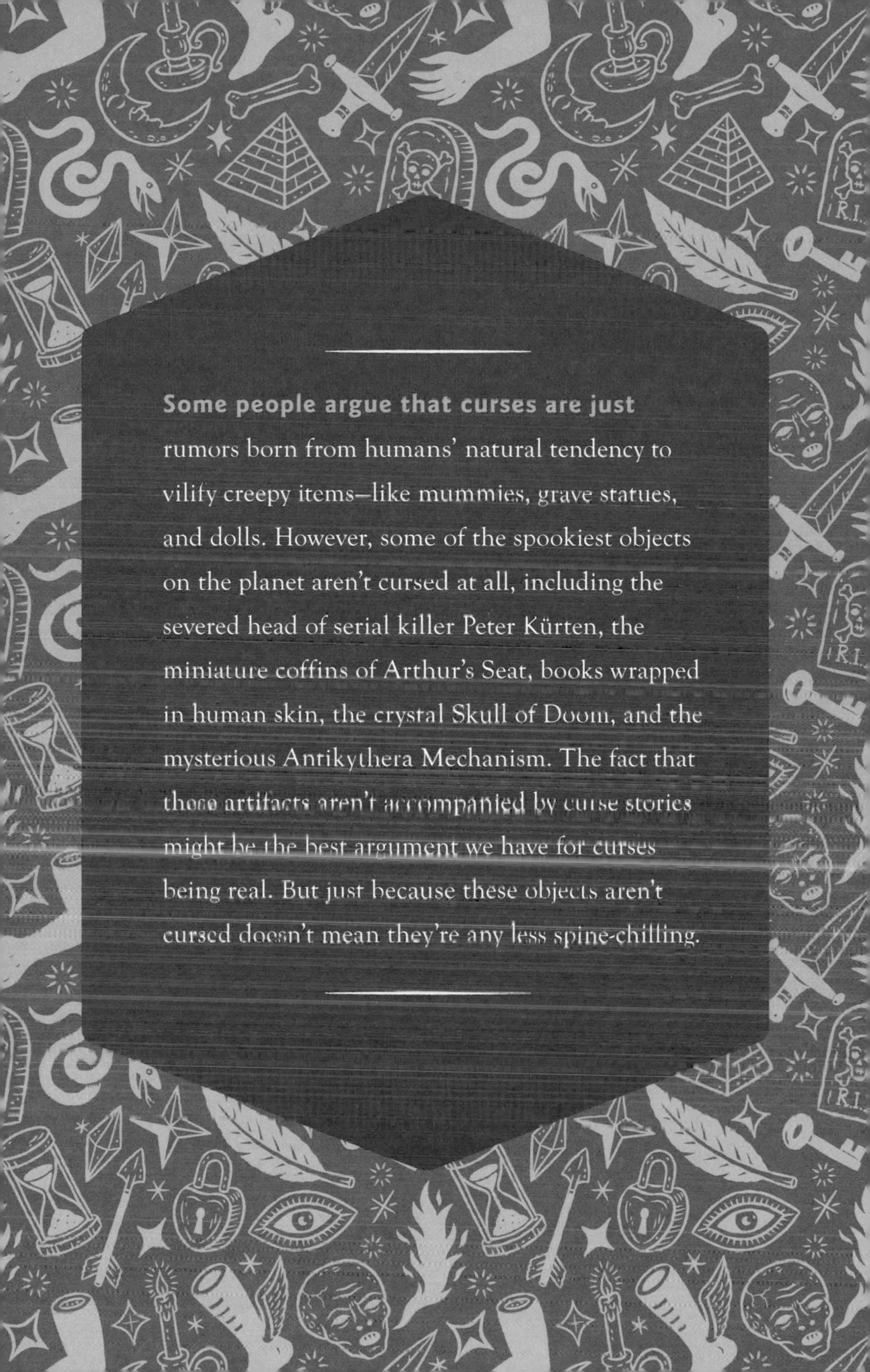

Some people argue that curses are just rumors born from humans' natural tendency to vilify creepy items—like mummies, grave statues, and dolls. However, some of the spookiest objects on the planet aren't cursed at all, including the severed head of serial killer Peter Kürten, the miniature coffins of Arthur's Seat, books wrapped in human skin, the crystal Skull of Doom, and the mysterious Antikythera Mechanism. The fact that these artifacts aren't accompanied by curse stories might be the best argument we have for curses being real. But just because these objects aren't cursed doesn't mean they're any less spine-chilling.

The Mummified Head of the Düsseldorf Vampire

BIRTHPLACE:
MÜLHEIM AM RHEIN, GERMANY

YEARS:
1883–1931

NUMBER OF KÜRTEN'S VICTIMS:
UNKNOWN (CONVICTED OF NINE MURDERS AND SEVEN ATTEMPTED MURDERS)

CURRENT LOCATION:
RIPLEY'S BELIEVE IT OR NOT!, WISCONSIN DELLS, WISCONSIN

It's the mummified, decapitated head of a serial killer known as the Düsseldorf Vampire. If anything's cursed, this object would be. But not a single legend, anecdote, or claim of a curse orbits this thing. It's like even curses don't want to be associated with it. And not only is it not cursed, it's freely available for you to visit.

Peter Kürten was born in 1883 in Mülheim am Rhein, Germany. He had an abysmal upbringing, crammed into a one-room house with twelve siblings and an alcoholic, abusive, incestuous, rapist father, in whose footsteps Kürten unfortunately followed. If the human race collectively found something abominable, Kürten found it embraceable — arson, rape, pedophilia, bestiality, and murder.

Kürten's rampage didn't start in earnest until 1929 in Düsseldorf. Most of his victims were women and girls, although some were men. Eventually, one of his victims who survived their encounter knew his address and told the authorities. Kürten was still able to elude them for a while, but when it became obvious that his time as a free monster was nearing an end, he advised his wife to turn him in and collect the reward money. Every dark heart has a silver lining.

He was officially tried for nine murders and seven attempted murders, although he confessed to seventy-nine offenses that also included assaults and even more murders

than he was tried for. You had a one in four chance of surviving an encounter with Kürten, but a zero in zero chance of escaping that encounter unviolated or unmaimed.

His weapon of choice was a hammer, but he got his Stokerian nickname from his obsession with blood. He found his victims' red stuff erotic and would drink it. It's rumored that his last words prior to bending before the guillotine were to the prison doctor. He said: "After my head is chopped off, will I still be able to hear, at least for a moment, the sound of my own blood gushing from the stump of my neck? That would be the pleasure to end all pleasures."

He was caught in 1930, tried, found guilty quicker than you can wipe something disgusting off your hands, and then executed in Düsseldorf in 1931. But he was such a monster that doctors had to crack his skull open and have a look inside. Because no way could Peter Kürten have an ordinary brain. It must have sharp teeth and eyeballs. It must be green and chitinous. But no – forensic analysis revealed it to be a regular human brain. Like yours and mine.

And the head that held that brain is still preserved and accessible to the public today. To see this artifact, you don't have to dig deep into the forensic archives of the Düsseldorf police station. You don't have to grave-rob a prison cemetery. You just have to go on a family vacation to Wisconsin Dells.

Wisconsin Dells is mostly T-shirt, souvenir, and fudge shops. And in any tourist town like that, you know there's a Ripley's Believe It or Not! museum nearby. And that's where the head of the Vampire of Düsseldorf is on display, ninety years after it met the cold edge of steel.

To see it, head to the vampire exhibit, which features a statue of Vlad the Impaler, a vampire killing kit, and all other kinds of fun with fangs. On the back wall of the exhibit is a hidden tunnel with the words "The Darker Side of Ripley's" spray-painted on it. Inside the tunnel and up a spiral staircase is a small room. In it is a mannequin in a tub of blood representing Elizabeth Báthory, a sculpture depicting a witch being burned at the stake made out of angel hair pasta, the chest of an English warlock, and, in a glass case framed in a wooden guillotine, the head of Peter Kürten. It is suspended on a hook and slowly rotates.

The head looks as if it has been peeled in two halves like banana skin. Inside each half is a hollow cavity where the very normal (biologically, at least) brain had been. Also bisected are the spinal cord, sinuses, and teeth. The skin wrapped around the face is finely preserved down to the nostril hairs and eyelashes. The eye sockets are hollow and black. You could almost match the head to the photograph of Kürten beside it.

So how did this revolting lump of mummified flesh find itself in a family attraction in a Great Lakes state? After World War II, it came into the personal collection of Arne Coward, an antiques dealer in Hawaii who collected instruments of torture – thumb screws, tongue tearers, executioner swords. If it was made to inflict pain, he wanted it in his living room – and Kürten's hollow head fit right into that theme. In 1979 Coward died, and his collection was auctioned. Ripley's bought the head and installed it in the Wisconsin Dells museum in 1990, where you can see it spinning today.

And though you won't be cursed by being in such close proximity, you will be haunted by it for the rest of your life.

The Mitchell-Hedges Crystal Skull

ORIGIN: NINETEENTH-CENTURY EUROPE	**ALSO KNOWN AS:** SKULL OF DOOM, SKULL OF LOVE
CLAIMED ORIGIN: PRE-COLUMBIAN BELIZE	**CURRENT OWNER:** BILL HOMANN
NOTABLE OWNERS: F. A. MITCHELL-HEDGES, ANNA MITCHELL-HEDGES	**DIMENSIONS:** 6" X 6" X 8", 11.5 POUNDS

It's a life-sized crystal skull supposedly pulled from the ruins of a Mayan temple. It's said that it can focus death beams on its victims. It inspired the first bad Indiana Jones movie. Of course it should be cursed. But it's not. In fact, these days it's called the Skull of Love.

Frederick Arthur Mitchell-Hedges was a British explorer in the early twentieth century. He was obsessed with lost cities and forgotten civilizations and spent most of his adventuring in Central America. He was a bit of an aggrandizer when it came to his exploits, though. He claimed to have discovered Atlantis, the Cradle of Civilization, and entire heretofore-unknown peoples. But the most famous and enduring claim associated with Mitchell-Hedges originated not from his own tales, but from those of his daughter, Anna.

According to Anna, when she was a teenager back in the 1920s, she accompanied her father during an expedition to the ruins of the pre-Columbian city of Lubaantun in British Honduras (now Belize). In that ancient city, Anna herself found the crystal skull beneath the wreckage of an altar. The skull measured about six inches wide, six inches tall and eight inches long and weighed a little more than 11.5 pounds. It had a detachable jaw but was otherwise a single beautiful hunk of quartz crystal.

Her father didn't talk much about it. He gave it the name Skull of Doom and claimed that it was thousands of years old and had been used by Mayan priests to will death on their enemies. That's about it. He even removed all mention of it from later versions of his memoirs. But after his death in 1959, Anna spent her life making that enigmatic crystal cabeza a paranormal celebrity. And she was successful — it's up there with Stonehenge as an icon of the strange.

Hypotheses have swirled in greater and greater orbits of credibility about the origin, purpose, and powers of the skull. Besides Mitchell-Hedges's story of it being a supernatural weapon wielded by holy men, others have suggested that it is extraterrestrial in origin. That the artifact is from Atlantis. That it's actually a computer. That it was used in rituals by the Knights Templar. That it causes visions. That it predicted the assassination of John F. Kennedy. That Satan made it (this theory courtesy of Church of Satan founder Anton LaVey himself when he paid it a visit). But in spite of all those theories and the evocative name Mitchell-Hedges gave it, the

spooky artifact doesn't have a reputation for being cursed, although one magazine really tried to give it that reputation.

The March 1962 issue of *Fate* magazine included an article by John Sinclair titled "Crystal Skull of Doom." In it, Sinclair tells a series of stories about purported victims of the skull. For instance, the Zulu witch doctor who mocked it and was then killed by a lightning bolt from a cloudless sky. And the photographer who made fun of it as he photographed it and then died in a car accident afterward. And then the two different occasions where people said disparaging things in the skull's presence and were punished with heart failure. Sinclair even hints that it was the cause of Mitchell-Hedges's demise, as well. The Skull of Doom's feelings are apparently easily hurt. The article stated that Mitchell-Hedges begged his daughter to bury the skull with him so that its evil would die, too.

However, the events listed in the article were either untrue or impossible to corroborate. There's also the fact that Anna lived to the age of one hundred despite the Skull of Doom being her roommate for almost her entire century of life. She even outright said that not only was the skull not cursed, it had healing properties, and that all the Skull of Doom talk from her father was him joking around. Later in its public life, it was rebranded as the Skull of Love. You can't have a cursed object called the Skull of Love. Sorry.

Since that time, various scientific tests have been performed on it and experts have analyzed it to various conclusions. But it was the skull's paper trail that finally did in its reputation as a pre-Columbian artifact with supernatural powers. According to the records, F. A. Mitchell-Hedges bought it at auction in London in September of 1943 for £400 from an art dealer named Sydney Burney. Most believe that the skull dates to the nineteenth century and that it is of European origin.

Since Anna's death in 2007, the Skull of Love has been kept by her widower Bill Homann, whom she married five years before her death. He maintains Anna's story of its discovery in the ruins of Lubaantun and brings it out for the occasional exhibit or television show.

Since the artifact is still in private hands, it's difficult for most of us to see in person. However, a skull of similar age and similarly murky provenance can be found in the Americas section of the British Museum in London. Like the Mitchell-Hedges skull, this one was also bought at auction. It has been in the British Museum collection and almost constantly on display since 1897, due to its popularity. Experts believe that this skull is not only older than the Mitchell-Hedges skull, but that the former was the model on which the latter was based. The main differences between the two are that the features of the British Museum skull are less refined and its jaw is not detachable.

Interestingly, the British Museum crystal skull is still kept in the gallery of American artifacts – albeit at quite a distance from the legitimate ones. It's almost hidden in a corner near the bathrooms, and its placard states apologetically:

Rock crystal skull
Late 19th century AD

It was originally thought to have been Aztec, but recent research proves it to be European.

The Miniature Coffins of Arthur's Seat

PLACE OF ORIGIN:	CURRENT LOCATION:
ARTHUR'S SEAT, EDINBURGH, SCOTLAND	NATIONAL MUSEUM OF SCOTLAND
YEAR DISCOVERED:	ALSO KNOWN AS:
1836	MURDER DOLLS

Seventeen tiny wooden coffins with seventeen tiny wooden corpses inside. Sounds like they might be voodoo dolls, or poppets. Maybe the key elements of a curse ritual, small props prepped for throwing into a fire, burying in the ground, or hiding in a cave to curse some unsuspecting individual who has wronged the spellcaster. However, while these seventeen cadavers in caskets are assuredly creepy, they're not cursed objects. Somehow.

They've been called Lilliputian coffins, fairy coffins, and coffin dolls, all of which feel right. Each wooden coffin is rough-hewn and about three inches long, with tiny bits of tin decorating the lids. The lids are removable, although they must be pried off; they are nailed down with small pins and other bits of metal. Inside each is a diminutive wooden figure, some naked and some with clothes stitched together from scraps of patterned cotton. Some are missing arms, and their eyes . . . are . . . all . . . open. Again, creepy, but not cursed. And most definitely mysterious.

In 1836, a small group of boys was playing on the slopes of Arthur's Seat in Edinburgh, Scotland. Geologically, Arthur's Seat is an extinct volcano. Mythically, it is offered as one of the possible sites of King Arthur's Camelot. Literarily, it's mentioned in Mary Shelley's *Frankenstein* and Jules Verne's *The Underground City*. Practically, it's an exhilarating place to explore and hike and take in the views.

The young Scottish lads just wanted to play, maybe find some rabbits. Little did they know they were about to make a discovery that would perplex researchers and historians for the next two centuries. At some point, one of them dislodged a blockade of stones to find a small recess in the rock. Inside that tiny cave were the seventeen tiny coffins, set up in two stacks of eight each, with the seventeenth coffin balanced across the pair of stacks.

And that . . . is most of what we know about them. To this day, nobody knows for sure what these miniature coffins represent, why they were placed at Arthur's Seat, or who made them. But there are theories. There are always theories.

For instance, some thought these were symbolic burials for people who had died in foreign lands or at sea, drawn from the traditions of either ancient Saxons or sailors. Some thought they were the opposite of cursed objects, lucky charms, and that the recess where they were found was a

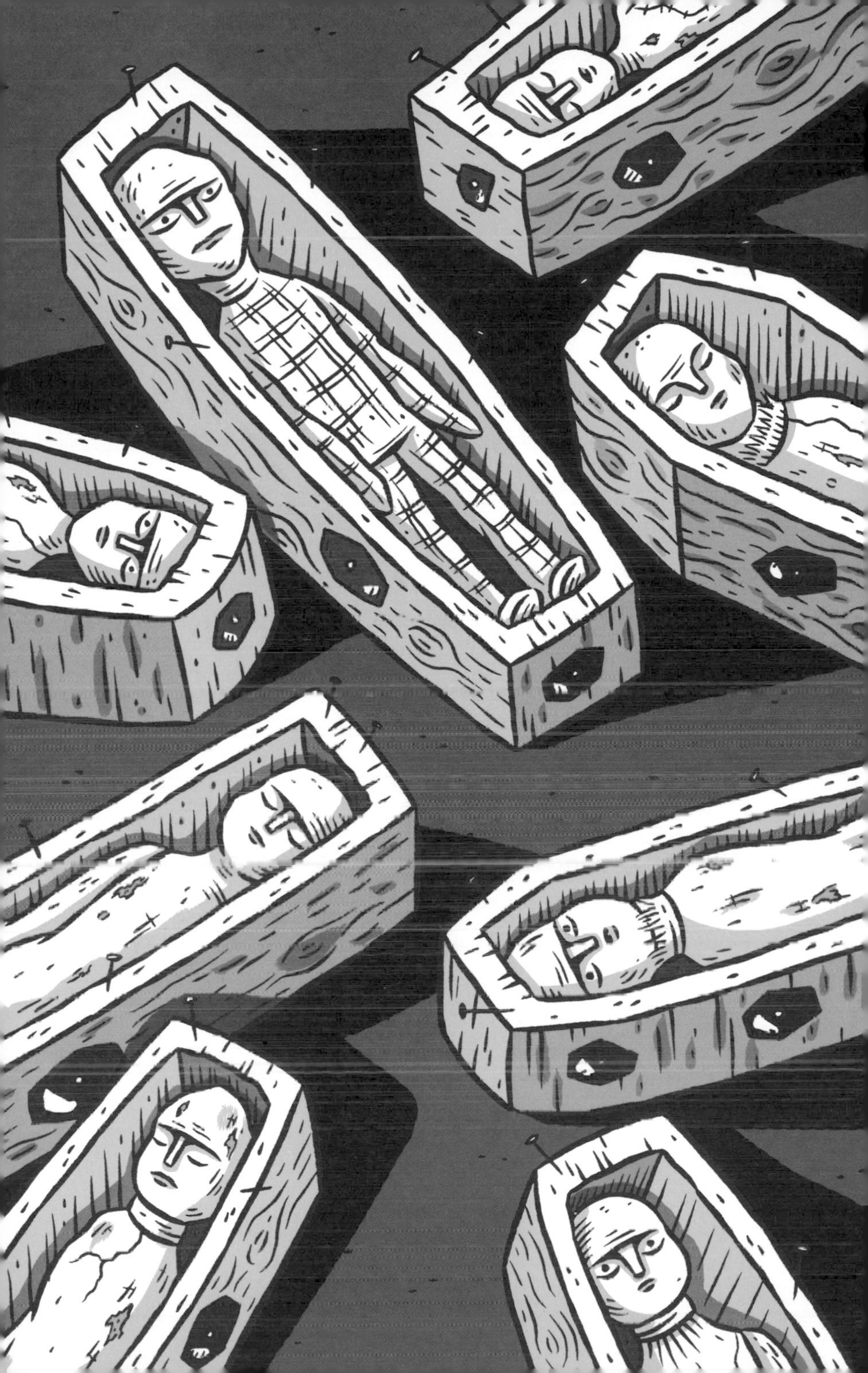

miniature warehouse for storing the stock for selling later. One more recent theory is that they were symbols from an early-nineteenth-century labor rebellion.

And, yes, a theory circulated right after their discovery that these were implements of witchcraft or demonology seeded into the mountain. So they got close to being dubbed cursed objects, but unfortunately, that theory never really took off. Besides, Scotland already has its own version of voodoo dolls: clay-bodies (or clay-corpses). Clay-bodies are figures molded out of clay that are placed in or under running water to be worn away, harming their victims as they disintegrate.

Eventually, a much more interesting theory emerged. When the boys first found the coffins, naturally they played with them, throwing the small toys in the air and at each other exactly as you'd expect children in the wild to do. The miniature coffins that survived the roughhousing were bought by private collectors and disappeared from public view until 1901. In that year, eight of the original seventeen coffins were donated to the National Museum of Antiquities of Scotland and then made their way to the National Museum of Scotland, where you can still see them on display today, more than one hundred years later.

In the 1990s, a detailed examination of the objects was undertaken by the museum. Researchers determined that they were probably carved by a single person (although they couldn't rule out two people) and that the coffins were most likely carved by cobbler tools. Also, the figures seemed to have been repurposed, because not all fit inside the coffins (hence the amputated arms) and their open eyes indicated that they weren't originally carved to be corpses. Possibly they were meant to be soldiers. Perhaps most interesting, the researchers dated the fabric to the early 1830s, which means the decaying figures had been almost brand-new when they were found.

This dating launched the idea that the miniature coffins were connected to one of the most infamous events in Scottish history: the Burke and Hare murders. In 1828, over the course of ten months, two men named William Burke and William Hare went on a murder spree, killing men, women, and children for the specific purpose of selling the fresh cadavers to Dr. Robert Knox of the Royal College of Surgeons of Edinburgh. He used them to perform dissections during a time when legitimate medical cadavers were hard to come by.

Two men named William Burke and William Hare went on a murder spree, killing men, women, and children for the specific purpose of selling the fresh cadavers.

Eventually the murders were discovered, and Hare turned on Burke. The latter was hanged for his crimes and then, ironically, dissected as a medical cadaver. Today, his skeleton and a notebook made of his skin are on display at the Anatomical Museum at the University of Edinburgh. A card case also made from his skin is on display at the shop of a local ghost tour operator called the Cadies and Witchery Tours. That's three more artifacts that should be cursed but aren't.

The number of bodies delivered to Dr. Knox by the two Williams was seventeen (depending on who's doing the math). The first was a natural death that gave Burke and Hare the idea of selling bodies, and the other sixteen were their murder victims. Which gives us seventeen bodies just a few years before the seventeen miniature coffins were made.

That means maybe, just maybe, that cave in the face of Arthur's Seat contained a private memorial for the seventeen bodies that Burke and Hare helped destroy and desecrate. And maybe, just maybe, since William Hare was exonerated for his part in the crimes by turning in his companion, they were made out of guilt by one of the murderers.

At the very least, that's a much more interesting theory than a curse, anyway.

Hollywood Hexes

Although cursed objects are relatively rare in real life, they power the plots of a massive percentage of movies. In many cases, these cursed items are the stars of the movies rather than mere props.

You could name almost any horror movie at random, and it would probably feature a cursed object. Like the video tape from *Ringu* (1998). The mirror in *Oculus* (2013). In 1987, *Hellraiser* introduced us to the Lament Configuration puzzle box. A coat button was cursed in *Drag Me to Hell* (2009). There's the video game in *Brainscan* (1994). The Necronomicon book in the Evil Dead trilogy (1981–1992). Another cursed book in *Scary Stories to Tell in the Dark* (2019). Everything in the cabin basement in *Cabin in the Woods* (2011). Every mummy in every mummy movie ever made. The gold cross in *The Fog* (1980). The 1958 Plymouth Fury in *Christine* (1983). Sheet music in *Deathgasm* (2015). And the lamp in *Amityville Horror 4: The Evil Escapes* (1989).

But horror movies aren't the only reliable genre for cursed objects. Fantasy adventures need them, too. In 2003, *Pirates of the Caribbean: The Curse of the Black Pearl* kicked off a franchise full of cursed ships and cursed treasure. Starting in 2001, the film adaptions of the Harry Potter books featured plenty of cursed objects, most notably the Horcruxes in the last two movies, *Harry Potter and the Deathly Hallows Part I* and *Part II* (although you could argue they're actually possessed). Jim Carrey found the cursed mask of Loki in 1994's *The Mask*. Indiana Jones chased down the Ark of the Covenant in *Raiders of the Lost Ark* (1981). The board game (and later video game) in the Jumanji movies. And then, of course, there's the One Ring of the Lord of the Rings trilogy (2001–2003), the one cursed object to rule them all.

The Skin Book of James Allen

PLACE OF ORIGIN:	CURRENT LOCATION:
BOSTON, MASSACHUSETTS	BOSTON ATHENAEUM, BOSTON, MASSACHUSETTS
YEAR CREATED: 1837	AUTHOR ALIASES: GEORGE WALTON, JONAS PIERCE, JAMES H. YORK, BURLEY GROVE
OCCUPATION OF JAMES ALLEN: HIGHWAYMAN	

I'm convinced that the term "anthropodermic bibliopegy" was invented so that people wouldn't have to talk about the concept of "books bound in human skin." Heck, the term might have been invented so people couldn't say it at all (it's pretty hard to say). But books bound in human skin aren't fiction. They weren't invented for horror stories. They aren't the product of deranged serial killers. And none of them are cursed.

Books bound in human skin can be found in libraries and museums around the world. Doctors used to bind books in skin. For instance, the Mütter Museum in Philadelphia has a set of three books from the late 1800s bound in the skin of a woman named Mary Lynch, who died from trichinosis. At Harvard University's Houghton Library in Cambridge,

Massachusetts, is another human-bound book, this one also from the late 1800s. It's a French meditation on life after death called *Destinies of the Soul*, and it's bound in the skin of a female patient who died of a stroke and whose body went unclaimed. Wrapping a book about the soul in bits of human husk has a certain poetry to it. The Wellcome Library in London has another nineteenth-century example of anthropodermic bibliopegy, a book on female virginity, this one also bound in the skin of a female patient whose body went unclaimed. Interest in binding books in human skin peaked in the nineteenth century, which tracks when you consider the Victorian obsession with death and the macabre.

Even more common than books bound in medical-cadaver hide are books bound in criminal hide. Many executed murderers or convicts who died in jail got their skin stretched around a book. We talked about what happened to the skin of the murderer William Burke in the previous entry (see page 209). Farther south, in London, there's a ledger bound in the skin of John Horwood, the first person hanged in Bristol Gaol. That book is in the Bristol Museum these days. A seventeenth-century book about Father Henry Garnet, a Jesuit priest executed for his role in the attempted assassination of King James I – known as the Gunpowder Plot – is supposed to be wrapped in his own skin. That volume is currently in private hands (that I hope get washed frequently).

Perhaps the most famous specimen of anthropodermic bibliopegy is the biography of the highwayman James Allen. Born around 1809, James Allen was an orphan who grew up on the streets of Boston. His first incarceration was at the age of fifteen for stealing a bolt of cloth, and from then on, he was a thief and a highwayman. His catchphrase, like most highwaymen of the day, was "Your money or your life." At some point in the winter of 1833–34, though, he highway'd the wrong man. Allen robbed a coach on the Salem Turnpike carrying one John Fenno. Despite the pair of pistols that Allen leveled at the traveler, Fenno put up a fight. So Allen shot him. Fortunately, the bullet only grazed Fenno, and Allen took off on his horse and lived to thieve another day.

Back at his place in Boston, Allen had no idea that he was suspected of the attempted robbery. He'd robbed travelers plenty of times before without getting caught. However, he soon grew suspicious that the police were zeroing in on him, so he made plans for a getaway. Just was he was about to board a boat for the West Indies, the authorities captured him.

In February 1834, Allen was convicted and sentenced to twenty years of hard labor at the Massachusetts State Prison. After a failed suicide attempt (the suspenders he'd wrapped around his neck broke, leaving him unconscious on the floor of his cell), he escaped and returned to a life of crime, a life that quickly yielded him a knife buried three inches into his head. According to the account that's now wrapped in his skin, he received this injury while defending a woman from being robbed. He was soon back in prison.

At that point, Allen caught tuberculosis, which had been making the rounds at the prison, and his thin jail cot became his deathbed. At some point Fenno visited Allen in jail, and some think he encouraged Allen to write down his life story as a deterrent for future criminals. Whatever his reason, Allen decided to do just that, enlisting the warden as his transcriber. Allen had two dying wishes. The first was that the warden take the narrative, make two copies, and bind them in Allen's skin after his death. His second wish was that one of those copies be delivered to John Fenno. The warden agreed.

Allen was able to narrate most of his life for transcription, although his work was left unfinished when he died on July 17, 1837, just shy of his thirtieth birthday. The warden was true to his word and had at least one copy bound in Allen's own skin. And you can see proof of that today at the Boston Athenaeum.

The library believes they own the Fenno copy; the whereabouts of the other are unknown, if it exists. The James Allen skin book that does exist is whitish-gray and supple. On its front cover is a black label with gold writing that states: *Hic liber Waltonis cute compactus est*. That translates to: "This book is bound in Walton's skin" (George Walton being one of Allen's many aliases). Other than that Latin phrase, nothing about the book gives any clue that it's covered in human leather.

And that is probably the book's most striking feature: its apparent normalcy. In fact, it's difficult to tell human leather from animal leather when it's that old. And that's true of many specimens of anthropodermic bibliopegy, some of which might be fakes and some of which might not have even been discovered yet. There could be many more out there, masquerading as mere cow- or goat-skin books.

And maybe one day, we'll find a cursed one.

The Antikythera Mechanism

ORIGIN: UNKNOWN	PLACE DISCOVERED: AEGEAN SEA, NEAR ANTIKYTHERA
AGE: 2,000 YEARS	CURRENT LOCATION: NATIONAL ARCHAEOLOGICAL MUSEUM, ATHENS, GREECE
YEAR DISCOVERED: 1900	

When you pull a strange object from an ancient sunken ship, there's good reason to believe that the object might be cursed — at the very least because it's been recovered from the sodden remains of a tragedy. But it's especially suspicious when said object is a thousand years ahead of its time. I'm referring to the Antikythera Mechanism, but it is not at all cursed. Historians and scientists think they know what the Antikythera Mechanism is, and that knowledge only makes its existence more baffling: it's a 2,000-year-old computer.

In 1900, sponge divers off the coast of the Greek island of Antikythera discovered the wreck of an ancient Roman ship. It was full of treasure: bronze and marble statues, jewelry, and coins. Experts believe the wreck dates to between 80 and 50

BCE. It was an amazing find, and within months, efforts were in place to recover the hoard from the fish forest below. Over the ensuing years the objects were dredged up, dried off, and delivered to the National Archaeological Museum in Athens, where they were cleaned and preserved and studied. So interesting were the rest of these treasures that it wasn't until 1951, fifty years after it was pulled from the sea, that somebody took a real interest in what seemed like a comparatively boring lump of corroded metal.

Closer examination revealed that hidden in all the corrosion and encrustment – courtesy of thousands of years of saltwater – were metal gears of meticulous craftsmanship, inscriptions in Greek, and exacting measurements, all of them revealing an object with much greater mechanical sophistication than was previously thought possible for the time. In fact, this technology wouldn't be invented until the fourteenth century, more than a thousand years after the date of the wreck – at least, according to the historical record as it then stood.

In its original state, the device had been the size of a shoebox, mounted in a wooden frame, and rather steampunk-looking with all of its bronze gears and faceplates. In its damaged state, in which it was found, the mechanism had broken into three parts, which were further broken down as it was cleaned and cataloged into an astounding eighty-two fragments.

The Antikythera Mechanism looks and functions a lot like an extremely complex clock. Except instead of terrestrial time, the mechanism tells celestial time. It features one hand for each of the five known planets at the time of its creation: Mercury, Venus, Mars, Jupiter, and Saturn, plus the sun and moon. A spinning black and silver sphere showed phases of the moon, and the mechanism at one time might have even included red and gold spheres representing Mars and the sun, respectively. Inscriptions and little dials marked the rising of stars, solar and lunar eclipses, and calendar days. It even featured instructions for using the device. Basically, the Antikythera Mechanism was an analog computer that could track the course of heavenly bodies hundreds of millions of miles out in space, some 2,000 years before a human being ever set foot on the closest one to Earth.

The device is unusual enough that its discovery launched some extremely weird theories, none of which include a curse. For instance, some believe that the Antikythera Mechanism is evidence of time travel — that a sloppy time-shifter from Earth's future dropped it into the timestream, where it ended up on a Roman boat that sank to the bottom of the Aegean Sea. Or that the mechanism is an extraterrestrial artifact,

left with a young human populace by benevolent beings of more advanced intelligence. That latter idea was propagated by Erich von Däniken in his popular 1968 book *Chariots of the Gods?*, in which he proposed that ancient astronauts from other worlds goosed the progress of Earth's foundational civilizations with gifts of technology.

A more prosaic theory is that it was merely invented and built by one of the greatest mathematical minds of the era, Hipparchus. He was perhaps the most accomplished astronomer of the ancient world. He was the first Greek to create accurate models that accounted for the motion of the moon and sun, he invented various instruments for observing the sky, and he is known as the father of trigonometry. Also important to the theory is the fact that he was of the same vintage as the machine.

Today, 120 years after its discovery, we still know only the bare minimum about the Antikythera Mechanism. We don't conclusively know who made it or where it came from or why it was on that ship, nor have we found similar devices from the time period. We don't even have all of its pieces, and some are undoubtedly still lying in the silt at the bottom of the Aegean Sea. Curiously, the Antikythera Mechanism hasn't inspired any curse stories — only awe and curiosity and wild theories about time travelers and alien beings.

Today, all eighty-two pieces of man-those-ancients-were-awesome are on public display at the National Archaeological Museum in Athens, where you can test your luck with it to see whether it might not be cursed after all.

The Curse in the Machine

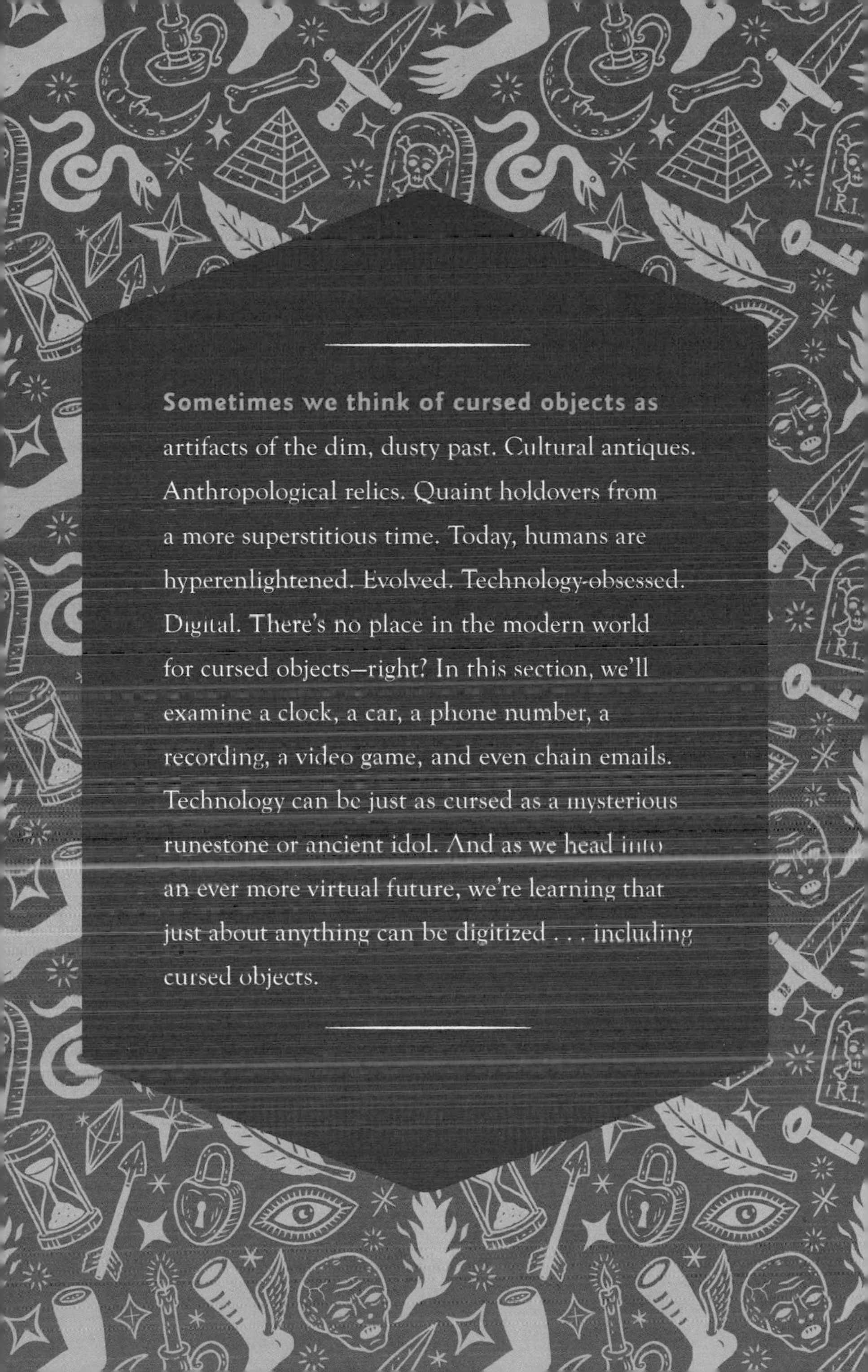

Sometimes we think of cursed objects as artifacts of the dim, dusty past. Cultural antiques. Anthropological relics. Quaint holdovers from a more superstitious time. Today, humans are hyperenlightened. Evolved. Technology-obsessed. Digital. There's no place in the modern world for cursed objects—right? In this section, we'll examine a clock, a car, a phone number, a recording, a video game, and even chain emails. Technology can be just as cursed as a mysterious runestone or ancient idol. And as we head into an ever more virtual future, we're learning that just about anything can be digitized . . . including cursed objects.

The Prague Orloj

PLACE OF ORIGIN:	YEAR MADE:
PRAGUE, CZECH REPUBLIC	1410
CREATORS:	**CURRENT LOCATION:**
MIKULÁŠ OF KADAŇ, JAN ŠINDEL	OLD TOWN HALL, PRAGUE, CZECH REPUBLIC

The precedent for cursed technology may have been crafted six hundred years ago in what is now known as Prague. The Prague Orloj, or Prague Astronomical Clock, is a giant, ornate piece of medieval machinery hanging on the side of the stone tower of Old Town Hall in Old Town Square in the capital of the Czech Republic.

It's a glorious monument to human accomplishment, to religion and science and art. Its shimmering dials tell Old Bohemian time, Babylonian time, Central European time, and star time. It tracks the zodiac, the calendar, and the position of the sun, moon, and stars. Every hour, when the clock tolls, it sets free a parade of twelve wooden apostle statues, each holding the implement of his martyrdom – an axe for the beheaded St. Matthias, a saw for the bisected St. Simon, and a knife and pelt for the skinned St. Bartholomew, to name a few. Meanwhile, other figures on the exterior of the Orloj come to life. A golden rooster crows. Figures of Vice

10
11

and Virtue nod their heads. There are angels and an astronomer, a philosopher, a vain man and a miser, among others. The oldest figure on the clock is a skeleton, which dates to the late fifteenth century and is sometimes called the Rattler, the Clicker, or *Kostlivec* in Czech. It represents death, and the figure nods sagely while ringing a bell in one hand and turning an hourglass in the other.

Walking through Old Town Square, Nutella-coated *trdelník* in hand, you can't help but gawp at it. And when it tolls the hour, you can't walk through the Old Town Square at all, since you'll invariably be shoulder-to-shoulder with people gazing up at its faces in awe. Maybe you'll hear a horologist squealing in delight or a travel guide pointing out the clock's various features. But you probably won't hear the guide tell their audience that the creator of the Orloj had his eyes gouged out or that the clock helped Nazis destroy the city.

The clock was made sometime around 1410 and was initially much plainer than its present state. It accrued its statues and ornamentation over the centuries. Astoundingly, some of the clock is still original, and many of its decorations have been in place for hundreds of years. The astronomical clock was originally created by master clockmaker Mikuláš of Kadaň and a priest and astronomer named Jan Šindel (interests: heaven and the heavens). It's then, at the moment of its unveiling, that the curse story begins.

According to the story, the leaders of the city were so impressed with this feat of art and science that they had the clockmaker's eyes gouged out with a hot poker so that he couldn't replicate it for another city. In retaliation, the clockmaker had somebody lead him up into the metal guts of the clock so that he could sabotage it (some say by throwing himself into the gears), cursing the clock and, by extension, the city. However, whenever this origin story is told, the clock's creators, Mikuláš and Šindel, aren't named. The story instead cites (and de-sights) one maker, Hanus Carolinum. Carolinum did indeed work on the clock, but not until about 1490, generations after its installation. But by the time the error was identified, the curse story had already stuck.

As for the nature of the curse, it varies by storyteller. Sometimes it's said that if anyone works on the clock or interferes with the clock, they will go mad or die. Other times it's said that if the clock ever stops, tragedy will befall the city. Yet other versions give the city a little bit of buffer, allowing that if the clock ever stops for a long period, the city will suffer.

I don't know about clockmakers going mad, but the Orloj has stopped here and there over the centuries. It's a complex mechanism that has been repaired and restored for different reasons, once because a firebomb hit it (we'll get to that in a minute). But the people of Prague kept fixing it and making it better and more beautiful, which is why today it's the oldest surviving medieval clock that still works.

But there are other myths about it. For instance, that the first chime of the day chases the goblins and ghosts away after their nightly revels. Another myth goes that if the curse is activated, the only way it can be averted is if a boy born on New Year's Day runs from the church to the clock before the Rattler stops nodding its skull.

So has anything bad happened to the people of Prague thanks to their cursed clock? Maybe. Do Nazis count? Some say that the Nazi occupation of Prague that began in 1939 occurred because the clock stopped working for a time. Adolph Hitler himself spent the night in Prague Castle after taking the country (then known as Czechoslovakia). He definitely ogled the Orloj, marveling at his stolen treasure.

Others say that it wasn't until the Prague Uprising in May 1945 that the curse finally delivered on its threats. During Germany's last gasps in World War II, the Czechoslovak resistance, bolstered by Soviet forces, attempted to liberate themselves from the Germans. During the three days of fighting, the Old Town Hall was badly damaged due to the aforementioned firebomb, as was the Orloj. It's said that at the very moment of damage, the tide turned against the Czechoslovak forces, although the Germans were eventually driven out when reinforcements from Russia arrived. Still, 1,700 Czechoslovaks died during that battle.

Today, after a 2018 renovation that took about nine months, the Orloj has been restored to its original state. Colors have been reverted to their authentic shades and metal gears replaced with wooden ones. It now looms even more medievally over Old Town Square, while sporting its modern antibird netting and ledge spikes. Because you can't be too careful with a giant cursed clock.

The Hungarian Suicide Song

COMPOSER:
REZSŐ SERESS

LYRICIST:
LÁSZLÓ JÁVOR

YEAR PUBLISHED:
1933

POPULAR PERFORMANCES BY:
PAUL ROBESON,
BILLIE HOLIDAY,
RICKY NELSON,
SARAH MCLACHLAN,
SINEAD O'CONNOR,
SARAH BRIGHTMAN

A song is, of course, neither a piece of technology nor quite what we think of as an object. It is art, it is expression. It's a series of vibrations in the air. But often, the manner in which that song is communicated – whether through the metal mesh of a microphone or an audio file – requires technology. And when that song is mass-produced and mass-delivered across radio and the Internet and television and physical media, it takes a whole network of complex technology. The upside to that technology is that it helps musicians' songs reach more listeners than they could have otherwise. The downside comes when that reach is extended for a song that causes its listeners to commit suicide. A cursed object that can be mass-produced and mass-consumed is a terrifying thing.

Rezső Seress was an extremely talented guy. He was a Hungarian pianist from Budapest who could play with one hand. A composer whose songs crossed oceans. A trapeze artist, for God's sake. He also had a pretty rough life. Most of it was spent in poverty, and during World War II, a chunk of it was lived in a Nazi labor camp with his family. His mother eventually died in that labor camp. But his melancholy started long before Hitler tainted the world.

He had one hit song, really: a piano tune in C minor that he wrote in Paris in 1932 called "Vége a világnak" (The World Is Ending). It was a doleful little ditty about the horrors of war and the uncertain future of mankind. He got it published about a year later. Maybe it was the Great Depression or the looming world war, but people seemed to dig it. And they dug it even more after a friend of his turned the song into a hit.

Poet and fellow Hungarian László Jávor elevated the song to new levels of attention when he rewrote Seress's lyrics to be more personal. Inspired by a recent breakup, Jávor made the song about the death of a lover and the desire of the song's narrator to die as a result. It included such woeful and evocative phrases, at least when translated, as "the shadows I live with are numberless" and "the black coach of sorrow has taken you" and "in death I'm caressing you." The new version was called "Szomorú vasárnap" (Sad Sunday).

In the United States "Sad Sunday" became "Gloomy Sunday" when songwriter Sam M. Lewis got his talented hands on it, and it was covered by everybody from Paul Robeson in 1936 to Billie Holiday in 1941. And despite those renditions being released under the title "Gloomy Sunday," Seress's signature work started to become known as the Hungarian Suicide Song. That's because it caused so many deaths that it got banned from clubs and radio airplay. Ostensibly.

In the late 1930s, some twenty suicides were tenuously linked to this song in both Hungary and the United States. The stories go that the song was referenced in suicide notes, that bodies were found beside gramophones still wailing the song, that victims were found clutching the crumpled sheet music in their cold, dead hands.

But the idea that this song was cursed took off when the BBC banned the Billie Holiday version from the radio during World War II. The official reason for the banning wasn't that it caused suicides necessarily, but that it was damned depressing and caused legitimate problems with morale during a time when there was a good fight to be fought.

Meanwhile, the popularity of that sad little song did little to elevate either Seress's state of mind or the levels of his bank account. As to the former, Seress believed that the success of "Gloomy Sunday" actually made him unhappy, because he didn't think he had it in him to write another hit like that one. As to the latter, he refused to cross the ocean to the United States to cash in on the popularity of the song and all the royalties he would have been due from it. Instead, he remained in both poverty and Budapest, playing piano at a restaurant called Kispipa, which was known for its patronage by misfits, the downtrodden, and the undesirable. The kind of place Billy Joel could only ever pretend to play at.

But what really put a coda on the story was the eventual fate of Rezső Seress. He too committed suicide, by jumping out the window of his apartment on January 11, 1968, not long after his sixty-ninth birthday. It was a Sunday.

Today, "Gloomy Sunday" still shows up in popular culture. An instrumental version of it is featured in Steven Spielberg's film *Schindler's List* (1993). The 2006 science fiction movie *The Kovak Box* used it as a plot device. The 2017 Netflix show *13 Reasons Why* referenced it.

It can also still be listened to, even if Spotify's algorithm doesn't ever suggest it. There are multiple versions to choose from. Like the Ricky Nelson version from 1958. Or the Sarah McLachlan and Sinead O'Connor renditions, both of which were released in 1992. Sarah Brightman sang it in 2000.

But maybe consult with your therapist before you listen.

James Dean's Porsche 550 Spyder

PLACE OF ORIGIN:	LOCATION OF CRASH:
STUTTGART, GERMANY	CHOLAME, CALIFORNIA
NICKNAME:	LAST KNOWN OWNER:
LITTLE BASTARD	GEORGE BARRIS
DATE OF CRASH:	CURRENT LOCATION:
SEPTEMBER 30, 1955	UNKNOWN

Had James Dean been part of the *Star Wars* generation, he would have known to listen to Obi Wan Kenobi. But James Dean died twenty-two years before *Star Wars* came out, so when he met the future Jedi Knight and knight of the British Empire Alec Guinness one fall evening in Hollywood in 1955, it was decades before the actor would play the wise, bearded Force guru.

Still, when Dean met Guinness, the elder actor was apparently already tapped into some mystical force. One week before Dean's death at the wheel of a very fast cursed object, the future Oscar-winning actor of *Bridge on the River Kwai* told the future Oscar-winning actor of *Rebel without a Cause* that if he got in that car he'd be dead in a week. Guinness was correct to the day. "A very, very odd, spooky experience," Guinness would call the moment more than two decades later during a 1977 interview with Michael Parkinson on the BBC talk show *Parkinson*.

James Dean was born in 1931 in Indiana. In 1951, he dropped out of UCLA to pursue acting. After a few commercials, walk-on movie roles, and television appearances, Dean filmed the three films that he is known for, *East of Eden* (1955), *Rebel without a Cause* (1955), and *Giant* (1956). He died before the latter two hit the screen. *Rebel without a Cause* garnered him a posthumous Academy Award and *Giant* a posthumous Academy Award nomination.

At the same time that his movie career was rocketing upward, Dean became fascinated by rocketing forward, and he started driving race cars competitively. Apparently, he was good at that, too, winning and placing regularly in races. Then he got a Porsche 550 Spyder. He had "Little Bastard" painted in cursive on its back end and the racing number 130 on its doors and hood. It was practically undriven when he proudly showed it to Alec Guinness that night in 1955.

On September 30, Dean was driving the tiny car on its maiden voyage from Los Angeles to Salinas to race it in the Salinas Road Race on October 1. In the passenger seat was his mechanic, Rolf Wütherich. Following him in Dean's Ford station wagon was Bill Hickman, a Hollywood stunt driver. The station wagon towed a trailer that was originally intended to carry the Little Bastard, before it was decided that Dean should log some more time behind the wheel before the races.

At 3:30 in the afternoon, he and his entourage were ticketed for speeding. They were going 65 mph in a 55 mph zone.

Two hours and fifteen minutes later, heading west on Route 466, a 1950 Ford Tudor coming from the opposite direction turned left onto Route 41. Dean smashed directly into the bigger and much heavier car, sending the Little Bastard cartwheeling into the gully.

Wütherich was badly injured but survived because he had been thrown from the vehicle. The twenty-three-year-old driver of the Tudor, Donald Turnupseed, exited his car with only minor injuries to his face. The twenty-four-year-old Dean, who was trapped in his vehicle as it went airborne, suffered multiple fatal injuries, including a broken neck.

The Spyder looked like balled-up aluminum foil on wheels. The wreck was ruled an accident.

Today Route 466 is now Route 46, and its intersection with Route 41 is called James Dean Memorial Junction. Dean went on to become an icon. The Spyder went on to become a cursed object, because we can't accept when a man as gifted as Dean isn't also gifted with indestructibility.

The wreck was divvied up. The engine and various other reusable parts went to another race car driver, Dr. William F. Eschrich. He installed the engine in his Lotus IX, and parts of the transaxle went into the racing car of his colleague and friend, Dr. Troy McHenry. About a year after Dean's death, both men crashed their cars in the same race. McHenry hit a tree and died, while Eschrich's car locked up and rolled over in a turn. He survived.

The rest of Little Bastard's carcass went to a man named George Barris, who customized the car for Dean originally, as well as some of the most famous vehicles on television – the Batmobile for the 1960s Adam West show, the Munster Koach, the Beverly Hillbillies' jalopy, and KITT from *Knight Rider*. Barris wanted to rebuild the Spyder but it was an impossible task, so he lent it to the National Safety Council, which toured the wreck around the country as a morbid safe-driving promo. According to Barris, he encountered many mishaps throughout the tour as a result of that car. He described how it caught fire, crushed a mechanic's legs, ripped the arm off a thief who wanted to steal the wheel, and killed a transport driver.

And then Dean's Spyder disappeared. According to Barris, it was being transported cross-country from Miami to Los Angeles in a sealed container, and when the container was opened at its destination, the car was gonzo. And it's never been seen since. Small pieces of the vehicle still linger in various private and museum collections, although, much like all the saint relics in Europe, the provenance isn't always verifiable.

In 2005, the Volo Auto Museum in Volo, Illinois, offered a $1 million reward to anyone who could find the Little Bastard. The offer was only taken up once, ten years later and sixty years after Dean's death. A man came forward and testified that he remembered seeing the hunk of death metal when he was six years old. Apparently his father and a group of men were hiding it behind a fake wall in a building in Whatcom County, Washington. The tip was never corroborated. The whereabouts of the Little Bastard to this day are unknown.

Although it might have taken one more victim. In 1981, Rolf Wütherich, the mechanic who survived the crash that killed Dean, died when he drunkenly drove his car into a house.

Back in 1955, the same year that James Dean died, he happened to film a short PSA for road safety that anybody can watch today on YouTube. After a bit of talking about how much scarier highways are than racetracks, Dean ended the bit with the line: "Take it easy driving. The life you might save might be mine."

0888-888-888

TELECOM ISSUER:
A1 BULGARIA

NOTABLE OWNERS:
VLADIMIR GRASHNOV,
KONSTANTIN DIMITROV,
KONSTANTIN DISHLIEV

CURRENT STATUS:
UNKNOWN

VICTIMS CLAIMED:
THREE

Today, our phone number is more important than any other number in our lives — far above our social security number or our driver license number or our zip code. That string of digits represented physically by the black pane of glass we all carry around in our pockets is used to give us access to unlimited information and connects us with everyone we know, love, or despise. If your phone number became cursed, it would be life-altering bad news beyond the usual bad news of learning you own a cursed object.

This is the story of a twenty-first-century cursed object: a mobile phone number. Which may seem weird to include in a book about cursed furniture and dolls and the like, but the more digital we become, the more technological advances are redefining the idea of an "object." For instance, a movie streamed digitally is still as much a movie as one watched on Blu-ray. If a cursed object can be built out of wood or metal or cloth, then why can't one be built out of code? But the important question is not a philosophical one but a question of results: can a digital artifact hurt or kill multiple people? The Bulgarian phone number 0888-888-888 seems to have.

This cursed object took out three victims in five years. The first was the former CEO of the Bulgarian telecom Mobitel, Vladimir Grashnov. In 2001, he died of cancer at age forty-eight after a long illness. At the time, nobody blamed it on his mobile phone number. Why would they? His phone number was a strange one, though. It was basically all eights: 0888-888-888. As the head of a telecom, he could presumably get whatever mobile number he wanted, and for some reason he chose that one. Some posit that it was because eight is a lucky number in Chinese numerology. Then again, maybe eight was his own personal lucky number. Or maybe he just wanted an easy number to remember. Still, when it happened, there were no rumors that connected the odd number to his untimely death.

A man named Konstantin Dimitrov was bequeathed it, ostensibly at his request. On December 6, 2003, Dimitrov was gunned down while dining at a high-end restaurant with his model girlfriend in Dam Square in Amsterdam. He was thirty-three years old. Of course, he was also a mob boss who happened to be checking on the Scandinavian arm of his massive, $500 million drug smuggling empire, so his death wasn't totally a surprise. It was attributed to the rival Russian mafia. His phone was, of course, on him when he died.

The next in line to get 0888-888-888 tied to his line was a real estate agent by the name of Konstantin Dishliev. Real estate is generally considered a safer occupation than being in the mob, but Dishliev's death was also swift and eerily similar to Dimitrov's. In 2005, Dishliev had just eaten dinner at an Indian restaurant in Bulgaria's capital city of Sofia when he was perforated by a storm of bullets. Turns out, Dishliev had a second business going outside of his open houses and furniture staging. He was trafficking cocaine. The theory goes that Dishliev was murdered after the authorities intercepted and seized $130 million of illegal white powder on its way to Colombia. He had become both a point of failure and a loose end for somebody.

It was at this point in the timeline of this ephemeral cursed object that people started connecting the dashes. Were these three men all cursed by the number that they shared? I know what you're thinking: Two of these men worked in violent, high-stakes crime. Their life expectancy was bound to be low regardless of their phone number. Still, it's weird.

Fortunately, according to the lore, the number was put in limbo for years by the police as part of the investigation into Dishliev's death. And, according to the story, when it was finally released, Mobitel pulled it from service. But according to a 2010 article in the *Daily Mail*, when questioned about the status of the cursed mobile number, the company's response was: "We have no comment to make. We won't discuss individual numbers."

Mobitel has rebranded as A1 Bulgaria, and mostly 0888-888-888 comes up these days when YouTubers make videos where they call the number to see what happens (sometimes they remember to stick the country code +359 in front of it, sometimes they don't). They always get the same canned message that the call can't be completed, much to their dramatized relief, even though the legend says nothing about calling the number, just owning the number.

The lore goes that the Bulgarian telecom took the number out of service to avoid more untimely deaths and/or bad press.

However, a simple reverse lookup reveals that the number does have an owner, one whose name I'll leave out of this entry, but who I assume is tired of getting prank phone calls. So, in a way, that might be the true curse of the 0888-888-888 number.

There are actually a handful of other cursed mobile numbers out there, and those same YouTubers like to call them all. In Thailand, it's supposed to be 999-9999. In Japan, 444-4444. Other Asian countries fear dialing 000-0000. In the U.S., we have that classic infernal recurring digit 666-666-6666. It seems human beings are just naturally suspicious of unnaturally repeating numbers.

The Berzerk Video Game Cabinet

PLACE OF ORIGIN:
CHICAGO, ILLINOIS

YEAR OF CREATION:
1980

CREATOR:
ALAN MCNEIL,
STERN ELECTRONICS

LAST KNOWN LOCATION:
FRIAR TUCK'S GAME ROOM,
CALUMET CITY, ILLINOIS

In 2019, video games earned $180 billion in revenue worldwide, making them the second largest entertainment sector, just below television. However, experts predict that video games will imminently pass the $200 billion mark and beat television to take first place. Everyone plays video games, from hardcore gamers with special chairs and headsets to senior citizens playing *Candy Crush* on the bus. Video games are a blast – which is why a cursed video game is particularly cruel.

Once upon a time (the 1980s), instead of downloading video games onto your devices from far-off servers, you went to the video games. They lurked in dark, dingy arcades in tall particleboard cabinets covered in neon graphics, looming over teenagers in jean jackets and baseball tees as if they knew that their technological descendants would soon rule the world. You stood up to play, meeting the low-resolution screen eye-to-eye, mashing buttons and yanking joysticks, seemingly dueling with the cabinet itself instead of battling 8-bit aliens or evading colorful ghosts. In the parlance of the times, it was awesome.

One such arcade was the medieval-themed Friar Tuck's Game Room in Calumet City, Illinois, right on the border with Indiana at the tip of Lake Michigan. One such cabinet in that arcade was a 1980 game called *Berzerk* . . . and that game cabinet was cursed.

This *Berzerk* cabinet was black with bright blue and red robots on its flanks. Its marquee touted the name of the game in red and chrome letters against a backdrop that was half starry sky and half a gridded orange and red horizon. It couldn't have looked more '80s.

The game was created by Alan McNeil, an employee of Stern Electronics in Chicago. It was based on a nightmare he had in which he was forced to fight a bunch of robots. After turning his nightmare into playable form, he named it after science fiction author Fred Saberhagen's *Berserker* novels.

In the game, you play a little green man with a gun trying to escape a maze full of flat-headed robots equipped with lasers. It was landmark for being one of the first video games to include a voice synthesizer, meaning that those flat-headed robots talked. In crunchy digital voices they shouted such phrases as, "The humanoid must not escape," and, when they killed you, "Got the humanoid, got the intruder." If a robot shot you, you died. If you touched a robot, you died. If you touched the walls of the maze, you died. And if you stayed on a maze screen for too long, a round, creepy, smiley-faced creature named Evil Otto would bounce onto the screen. And if he caught you, you would die. Evil Otto was based on a security chief named David Otto at one of McNeil's previous jobs. McNeil said the man would smile while he "chewed you out."

Finally, if you played the *Berzerk* cabinet at Friar Tuck's Game Room, you would die. At least, that's the story of what happened to three unlucky players in the '80s. The first victim was a teenager named Jeff Dailey. He was rocking the game hard enough that he'd earned two spots in the top score ranking. He died of a heart attack right there among the flashing screens and bloops and bleeps of the game cabinets. His high score? 16,660. However, many believe that this story is made up – an urban legend – and that there's no proof of this Jeff Daily and his Satanic score. And that's probably true.

But Victim #2 was very real. His name was Peter Burkowski. He was eighteen. And his fateful encounter with the

video game cabinet occurred in 1982, not long after Friar Tuck's grand opening that year. His story is similar enough to the Jeff Dailey story to imply that they are the same story. Burkowski also landed his initials in the top scores twice and then died of a heart attack. It happened as he quit *Berzerk* for another cabinet a few steps away. No sooner had he dropped a quarter in the slot of the new game than Burkowski dropped dead. According to a 1982 *Chicago Tribune* article, his autopsy revealed scarring on his heart. The condition was preexisting, and the conclusion was that the intensity of the game did his weakened heart in, as any rigorous activity would have done. The authorities investigated the *Berzerk* cabinet just in case but found no "electronic defects."

The third victim of the cursed video game was also very real, but his death diverges from the cabinet's heart attack M.O. (although cursed objects rarely have a consistent M.O.). In 1988, a group of teenagers, including Pedro Roberts and Edward Clark Jr. got into a fight at Friar Tuck's, and Roberts stabbed Clark in the chest. Clark died later in a nearby clinic across the state line in Indiana. Although official accounts don't detail what started the fight, the general story is that one of the teenagers left quarters on the *Berzerk* game to reserve his spot, and another player stole one of the quarters to play the game himself.

No other *Berzerk* game in the thousands of arcades across the country during that decade had a body count. There was something about this particular cabinet in Illinois. Of course, today we are familiar with the idea of people dying while playing video games. Usually it's during marathon gaming sessions, in which players game for days on end. Heart attacks can happen, as can dehydration. But in no other instance have video-game-related deaths clustered around not only a specific game, but a specific gaming cabinet.

In a final bizarre twist, Calumet City, Illinois is known for two distinct landmarks: a pair of round water towers, each of them painted with smiley faces . . . the exact visage of Evil Otto.

Friar Tuck's Game Room shut down in 2003, a victim to the advances in home video gaming technology. The fate of the *Berzerk* cabinet is at this time unknown.

Chain Emails

Following the advent of messaging platforms and social media, email feels stodgy. It has become the communication medium of business. A landfill of receipts and coupons and newsletters. But, man, it used to be such a joy.

In the early days of the Internet, logging on to your blocky desktop computer to discover an unread message sitting in your inbox was a fantastic experience. Life changing, really. Somebody had typed you an email, hours or minutes or seconds ago, and here it was for you to read. And you could respond instantly, without having to dig up a stamp or find a mailbox. It was the magic of having a summer camp pen pal amplified by the magic of the World Wide Web.

And then the chain emails came. Worse yet, the cursed chain emails came. Chain emails are emails written to convince recipients through either promises or threats to forward the same message to a designated number of friends and acquaintances. These friends and acquaintances, in turn, are exhorted or threatened to send it out themselves to a set number of people. The idea is that a single email can kickstart an exponentially growing chain of emails. The content of these emails can include promises of fortune ("For every person that you forward this email to, Microsoft will pay you $245.00"), charity opportunities ("The American Cancer Society will donate three cents to cancer research for everyone that gets forwarded this message"), notices of important information ("Hotmail needs to delete users and wants to make sure your account is active, so please forward this email to every Hotmail user you know"), and outright supernatural curses. We'll get to those.

To understand the history of chain emails, we have to start with chain letters. One of the first examples of a chain letter on record was in 1888, about the time when stamps and stationery had become close to throwaway cheap. The originator had good intentions: to raise money for a Methodist school for women missionaries in Chicago that was $16,000 in debt. They called it a "peripatetic contribution box." And, in fact, it worked well enough that others tried it.

That same year in Whitechapel, England, the Bishop of Bedford tried to use chain letters to defeat Jack the Ripper. He wanted to establish a Home for Destitute Women to protect them from the murderous night prowler and thought that what he called a "snowball collection" was a great idea for fundraising. However, the bishop ran into telephone-game problems; the donation address and amount needed were corrupted in the replication, and the letters became so numerous and error filled that they had to run newspaper advertisements to break the chain.

Chain letters reached their peak of ridiculousness in 1935, when those in the throes of the Great Depression turned to the practice out of desperation. There were entire chain letter brokerages set up, businesses dedicated completely to sending out chain letters. One such establishment in Ohio employed 125 people. The market quickly bottomed out, however, and eventually became the domain of con artists, who knew that with a little bit of wordsmanship and a few seed letters, they could pull in money for nothing.

And then came email, which made the scam even easier.

No longer did links in the correspondence chain have to painstakingly copy, address, and mail pieces of paper. All it took was clicking the Forward button. Now it was easy enough to do that pranksters could start a chain on a whim. And once started, chain emails were difficult to squelch.

When it came to cursed chain emails, it was like being able to send dozens of dybbuk boxes at a time to your enemies in mere seconds of server hopping. One cursed chain email threated that the ghost of a murderous child named Clarissa would bleed you to death in your sleep if you didn't forward it. Another claimed that Bloody Mary would come and mutilate your body if you didn't send the note to ten more people. Yet another introduced the ghost of a seven-year-old named Teddy with no eyeballs and a blood-stained face who threated to kill the recipient in their sleep if the message wasn't forwarded to twelve more people. There's also one about the ghost of Carmen Winstead, who was pushed down a well during a school fire drill. Here's how that one reads, complete with grammatical errors, according to Snopes.com:

> About 6 years ago in Indiana, Carmen Winstead was pushed down a sewer opening by 5 girls in her school, trying to embarrass her in front of her school during a fire drill. When she didn't submerge the police were called. They went down and brought up 17 year old Carmen Winstead's body, the neck broke hitting the ladder, then side concrete at the bottom. The girls told everyone she fell . . . They believed them.
>
> FACT: 2 months ago, 16 year old David Gregory read this post and didn't re-

> post it. When he went to take a shower he heard laughter from his shower, he started freaking out and ran to his computer to repost it, He said goodnight to his mom and went to sleep, 5 hours later his mom woke up in the middle of the night cause of a loud noise, David was gone, that morning a few hours later the police found him in the sewer, his neck broke and his face skin peeled off.
>
> If you don't repost this saying, "She was pushed" or "They Pushed her down a sewer" then Carmen will get you, either from a sewer, the toilet, the shower, or when you go to sleep you'll wake up in the sewer, in the dark, then Carmen will come and kill you.

There were plenty more that followed this same pattern with different spooks carrying out the curse. Like a killer clown. Or Scary Mary, who will come at you through a mirror if you don't forward the email. There's even one featuring a killer Mickey Mouse who will slit your throat, fork out your eyeballs, and stuff your body under your bed. These cursed chain emails often arrived under headings like: "This email has been cursed and once opened you must send it." Short descriptions of previous victims were usually appended to the end of the message.

These days, highly intelligent spam filters have saved our lives and our souls from most of these cursed digital objects. And most of us have shifted the bulk of our online communications to the aforementioned messaging platforms and socials, anyway.

But if history is any indication, you can't keep a cursed object buried for good. The cursed chain letter adapted to become the cursed chain email and that, in turn, has adapted to become the cursed SMS. Or the cursed Facebook post. Or the cursed tweet ("RT this in five seconds or your mom will die!"). And it turns out that the socials can circulate dubitable information even faster and on a larger scale than email.

On the other hand, it only takes seconds to retweet a cursed chain message . . . and what if it's true?

The Science of Cursed Objects

Here's a sentence I should have started the entire book with: there is scientific evidence that cursed objects are real.

Most of us are familiar with the placebo effect. That's when patients feel better because they believe they've been given a remedy to their ill, even when they haven't. The nocebo effect is kind of the opposite. Like the placebo effect, the nocebo effect is a medical term, one coined by Walter Kennedy in a scientific paper in 1961 (although he called it the "nocebo reaction"), six years after Henry Beecher introduced the placebo effect.

Basically, the nocebo effect is when a patient experiences negative side effects because they believe they've been given a remedy with negative side effects, even when they haven't. For instance, if the patient was told a pharmaceutical has the side effect of hallucinating purple bats, the patient hallucinates purple bats even if he or she was given a different pill without those side effects.

Instead of the powers of positive thinking, it's all about the dangers of negative thinking. The nocebo effect has similarities with the idea of voodoo death, a term created by a doctor named Walter Cannon in 1942. Voodoo death is when someone is scared to death after believing they've been cursed, basically. The death is psychosomatic, as is the nocebo effect.

Of course, I'm grossly simplifying the concept, but, still, it's easy enough to draw a parallel with cursed objects. If you think harm will come to you because of a cursed object, you (and/or your body) will find a way for that harm to happen.

Certainly, placebo and nocebo effects are still mysterious concepts in medicine, but they're backed by lots of evidence. Sometimes science and superstition high-five each other.

Epilogue

The Fear and Love of Cursed Objects

I was a little apprehensive when I started this project. But not because I would be visiting, researching, and writing about objects that are supposed to bring harm to those who merely show an interest in them. If a cursed object did me harm, so be it, but my real fear was that something bad would coincidentally happen to me over the year it took to write this book (after all, in any given year a person's chances of some misfortune are high), and this book would fuel some kind of false curse story. Especially if there was an obituary: "Author J. W. Ocker was killed in a freak Pringles can accident. He was in the middle of writing a book about cursed objects." That's pretty much exactly what happened to most of the people mentioned in this book.

But eventually that worry abated, and I fell in love with cursed objects. I've always enjoyed stories about cursed objects and I'd often visit them on my weird travels, even without an assignment. But what I grew to appreciate during this book journey was how powerful they are as starting points for stories. Folklore and campfire tales and legends are ephemeral, sounds spoken from the lips and disappearing into the air. But cursed objects can be held, hefted, examined. They can be put on display. Photographed. Loaned out. Worn. Juggled. Slept with. Transported. Held in the air. Sat on. It's the weight that gives their stories weight.

So I was surprised when I discovered that there are so few famous (or infamous) cursed objects. Especially when you compare them to, say, famous haunted buildings. In fact, what you hold in your hands might be the most complete list assembled to date.

I don't know why we don't have more well-known stories of cursed objects. Maybe it's because objects are easily lost, and their stories along with them. Maybe "cursed" as a concept isn't as trendy as "haunted" at the beginning of the twenty-first century, when ghost hunting has become an industry. Maybe, in a materialistic, capitalistic society such as ours, it's too transgressive to think of our possessions as bad.

But I still have my cursed bulldog. It's on a shelf in my office, between a skull-shaped bottle of Dan Aykroyd's Crystal Skull vodka and a yellow bathtub duck from a haunted castle I stayed at in Ireland. I call it the Cursed Cur because all the best cursed objects have dramatic names that sound like the second half of the title of a mystery novel.

One request: if I die under strange circumstances, please don't reference it in my obituary.

Selected Bibliography

For a complete list of references consulted, visit quirkbooks.com/cursedobjects.

I. Cursed Under Glass

The Hope Diamond

Kurin, Richard. *Hope Diamond: The Legendary History of a Cursed Gem*. New York: Collins, 2006.

Smithsonian Institution. "The Hope Diamond." Accessed November 2019. www.si.edu.

Ötzi the Iceman

BBC News. "Death Renews Iceman 'Curse' Claim." November 5, 2005. http://news.bbc.co.uk.

Hall, Stephen S. "Unfrozen." *National Geographic*, November 2011. www.nationalgeographic.com.

Māori Taonga

Chapman, Paul. "New Zealand Museum Tells Pregnant Women to Stay Away." *Telegraph*, October 12, 2010. www.telegraph.co.uk.

Mitira, Tiaki Hikawera. *Takitimu*. Wellington: Reed Publishing, 1972. www.nzetc.victoria.ac.nz.

The Tomb of Tutankhamen

Charleston, L. J. "Incredible True Story of the Life and Death of the 'Boy-King.'" *Herald Sun*, January 5, 2019. www.heraldsun.com.au.

Luckhurst, Roger. *The Mummy's Curse: The True History of a Dark Fantasy*. Oxford: Oxford University Press, 2012

A Curse Is Forever

Balfour, Ian. *Famous Diamonds*. New York: Antique Collectors' Club, 2008.

Lovejoy, Bess. "8 Supposedly Cursed Gems." *Mental Floss*, updated October 16, 2019. www.mentalfloss.com.

Murasama Swords

Baseel, Casey. "Scholars Confirm First Discovery of Japanese Sword from Master Bladesmith Masamune in 150 Years." *SoraNews24*, September 9, 2014. www.soranews24.com.

Yuhindo.com. "Sengo Muramasa." Accessed November 2019. yuhindo.com/muramasa.

The Unlucky Mummy

Eveleth, Rose. "The Curse of the Unlucky Mummy." *Nautilus*, April 10, 2014. www.nautil.us.

Luckhurst, Roger. *The Mummy's Curse: The True History of a Dark Fantasy*. Oxford University Press, 2012

The Ring of Silvianus

Chute, Chaloner William. *A History of the Vyne in Hampshire*. London: Simpkin, Marshall & Co., 1888.

Hendrix, Jenny. "'Cursed' Roman Ring May Be Tolkien's 'Ring to Rule Them All.'" *Los Angeles Times*, April 2, 2013. www.latimes.com.

This Book Is Cursed!

Boba, Eleanor. "You Have Been Warned: Book Curses (And Cursed Books)." American Bookbinders Museum blog, October 31, 2016. www.bookbindersmuseum.org.

Drogin, Marc. *Anathema! Medieval Scribes and the History of Book Curses*. Totowa, NJ: Allenheld & Schram, 1983.

II. Cursed in the Graveyard

The Black Aggie

Hunter, Marjorie. "Adams Memorial Draws Responses." *New York Times*, June 7, 1983.

Kelly, John. "'Black Aggie': From Baltimore to Washington." *Washington Post*, August 18, 2012. www.washingtonpost.com.

The Björketorp Runestone

Fotevikens Museum. "Björketorp runsten." Accessed November 2019. www.fotevikens-museum.se.

Steve's Travels & Stuff. "Bjorketorp Rune Stone." July 29, 2017. www.stevethings.wordpress.com.

The Tomb of Timur

Smith, Hendrick. "Debate Stirs in Shadow of Tamerlane Tomb." *New York Times*, June 2, 1974.

Tancl. "The Curse of Tamerlane." *Smart History Blog*, October 28, 2016. www.smarthistoryblog.com.

The Black Angel

Carroll, Joyce, and Allison Settles. "The Black Angel Monument." Iowa City: Document Services. Accessed November 2019. www.iowa-city.org.

Hogan, Suzanne. "How a Black Angel Statue in Iowa Went from Heartfelt Memorial to Spooky Legend." KCUR, October 20, 2016. www.kcur.org.

How to Curse an Object

BBC News. "'Cursing Stone' Found on Isle of Canna." May 20, 2012. www.bbc.com.

Thegoodishtraveler. "Nimbu Mirchi." *Atlas Obscura*, accessed November 2019. www.atlasobscura.com.

The Gravestone of Carl Pruitt

Henson, Michael Paul. *More Kentucky Ghost Stories*. Johnson City, Tenn.: Overmountain Press, 2000.

JasonB. "Anatomy of a Ghost Story: The Search for Carl Pruitt." *Cvlt Nation*, October 17, 2016. www.cvltnation.com.

The Bronze Lady

Ferri, Jessica. "The Bronze Lady: The (Other) Spooky Legend of Sleepy Hollow that You've Never Heard Of." *The Lineup*, October 24, 2017. www.the-line-up.com/.

Leary, Robyn. "Ghost Stories: The Other Legend of Sleepy Hollow." *New York Times*, October 29, 2000. www.nytimes.com.

Shakespeare's Grave

BBC News. "Bard's 'Cursed' Tomb Is Revamped." Updated May 28, 2008. www.news.bbc.co.uk.

Young, Sarah. "Radar Scan of Shakespeare's Grave Confirms Skull Apparently Missing." Reuters, March 24, 2016. www.reuters.com.

III. Cursed in the Attic

The *Crying Boy* Painting

Clarke, David. "The Curse of the Crying Boy." *Dr. David Clarke Folklore and Journalism*, accessed November 2019. www.drdavidclarke.co.uk.

Zarrelli, Natalie. "A Painting of a Crying Boy Was Blamed for a Series of Fires in the '80s." *Atlas Obscura*, April 21, 2017. www.atlasobscura.com.

The Baleroy Chair of Death

Foti, Kaitlyn. "Chestnut Hill's Baleroy Mansion's Many Ghost Stories." *Patch*, October 31, 2011. www.patch.com.

People Magazine. "Spirited Welcome." October 31, 1994. www.people.com.

The Dybbuk Box

Gornstein, Leslie. "A Jinx in a Box?" *Los Angeles Times*, July 25, 2004. www.latimes.com.

Levy, Lauren. "The Full Story on Post Malone and the Cursed Box" *Fader*, October 24, 2018. www.thefader.com.

The Basano Vase

Thegypsy. "The Curious and Deadly Tale of the Basano Vase." The Gypsy Thread, March 12, 2018. www.thegypsythread.org.

Puchko, Kristy. "10 Allegedly Cursed Objects." *Mental Floss*, February 22, 2016. www.

mentalfloss.com.

That Voodoo That You Do So Well

Armitage, Natalie. "European and African Figural Ritual Magic: The Beginnings of the Voodoo Doll Myth." In *The Materiality of Magic: An Artefactual Investigation into Ritual Practices and Popular Beliefs*, edited by Ceri Houlbrook and Natalie Armitage, 85–101. Oxford: Oxbow Books, 2015.

Rudolph Valentino's Ring

King, Gilbert. "The 'Latin Lover' and His Enemies," Smithsonianmag.com, June 13, 2012. www.smithsonianmag.com.

Ripley's Believe It or Not! "Rudolph Valentino's Cursed Ring Remains Locked in a Hollywood Vault." March 27, 2018. www.ripleys.com.

Robert the Doll

Key West Art & Historical Society. "Robert the Doll." Accessed November 2019. https://www.kwahs.org.

Robertthedoll.org. "A Boy & His Doll." Accessed November 2019. www.robertthedoll. org /a-boy-his-doll.

Busby's Stoop Chair

Minting, Stuart. "18th Century Murderer's Chair Continues to Captivate Supernatural Fans." *Northern Echo*, October 29, 2014. www.thenorthernecho.co.uk.

Wax, Alyse. "This Vintage Chair May Carry a Deadly Curse." *13th Floor*, October 2, 2015. www.the13thfloor.tv.

The Conjured Chest

Carter, Beth Caffery. "New Details about the Cursed Chest." Kentucky Historical Society, accessed December 2019. www.history.ky.gov.

Hudson, Virginia Cary. *Flapdoodle, Trust & Obey*, New York: Harper & Row, 1966.

IV. Cursed in Stone

The Little Mannie with His Daddy's Horns

Ludden, Kevin. "There's No Flies on Little Mannie." *Sun*, July 1991.

Prag, A. J. N. W. "The Little Mannie with his Daddy's Horns." In *The Materiality of Magic: An Artefactual Investigation into Ritual Practices and Popular Beliefs*, edited by Ceri Houlbrook and Natalie Armitage, 171–81. Oxford: Oxbow Books, 2015.

The Cursing Stone

BBC Cumbria. "Curse of the Cursing Stone." Updated March 19, 2006. www.bbc.co.uk.

Guardian. "They're Doomed." March 8, 2005. www.theguardian.com.

The Monogram of Patrick Hamilton

Museum of the University of St. Andrews. "Watch Your Step: The Curse of the 'PH.'"

Museum Collections Blog, June 12, 2018. www.museumoftheuniversityofstandrews.wordpress.com.

University of St. Andrews. "A Brief History of St. Salvator's Chapel." Accessed November 2019. www.st-andrews.ac.uk.

The Cursed Pillar

The Insider. "The Curse of the Haunted Pillar Continues." *Metro Spirit*, December 21, 2016. www.metrospirit.com.

Oster, Grant. "An Attempt to Debunk the Haunted Pillar of Augusta, Georgia." *Hankering for History*, updated December 18, 2016. www.hankeringforhistory.com.

No Cursed Stone Unreturned

Hayes, Cathy. "Blarney Castle Curse Dooms Canadian to Bad Luck." *Irish Central*, June 30, 2010. www.irishcentral.com.

Twilley, Nicola. "Slide Show: Rocks, Paper, Sinners." *New Yorker*, January 23, 2015. www.newyorker.com.

The Hexam Heads

Clarke, David. "Heads and Tales." *Dr. David Clarke Folklore and Journalism*, December 22, 2012. www.drdavidclarke.co.uk.

The Urban Prehistorian. "The Hexham Heads." January 27, 2014. www.theurbanprehistorian.wordpress.com.

The Amber Room

Blumberg, Jess. "A Brief History of the Amber Room." Smithsonianmag.com, July 31, 2007. www.smithsonianmag.com.

Nally, Richard. "Mysteries of the Amber Room." *Forbes*, March 29, 2004. www.forbes.com.

The Treasure of Cahuenga Pass

Alper, Joshua. "The Cahuenga Pass Treasure." *Southern California Quarterly* 81, no. 1 (Spring 1999): 89–116. www.doi.org.

Rasmussen, Cecilia. "Curse of the Cahuenga Pass Treasure." *Los Angeles Times*, January 23, 2000.

V. The Business of Cursed Objects

Annabelle the Doll and the Warren Collection

Genzlinger, Neil. "Lorraine Warren, Paranormal Investigator Portrayed in 'The Conjuring,' Dies at 92." *New York Times*, April 19, 2019. www.nytimes.com.

Warrens.net. "The Curse of the Devil Doll Housed in the Warrens Occult Museum." Accessed November 2019. www.warrens.net/annabelle.

John Zaffis Museum of the Paranormal

John Zaffis, Godfather of the Paranormal (website). "Museum." Accessed November 2019. www.johnzaffis.com.

Zaffis, John, and Rosemary Ellen Guiley. *Haunted by the Things You Love*. New Milford, CT: Visionary Living, 2014.

Zak Bagans's The Haunted Museum

ElGenaidi, Deena. "The Trickery and Silly Kitsch of a Supposedly Haunted Museum in Las Vegas." *Hyperallergic*, February 28, 2019. www.hyperallergic.com.

Zak Bagans' Haunted Museum. "About Zak Bagans's Haunted Museum." Accessed November 2019. www.thehauntedmuseum.com.

The Traveling Museum of the Paranormal and Occult

Newkirk, Greg. "The 'Bruised Man' of Friendsville: How a Chest Full of Haunted Artifacts Saved Me from Being Murdered." *Week in Weird*, November 24, 2016. www.weekinweird.com.

Traveling Museum of the Paranormal & Occult. "Attend an Exhibition." Accessed November 2019. www.paramuseum.com.

VI. Why Aren't These Objects Cursed?

The Mummified Head of a Vampire Serial Killer

Hintz, Charlie. "The Head of German Serial Killer Peter Kürten in Wisconsin Dells." *Cult of Weird*, August 14, 2017. www.cultofweird.com.

White, Nic. "Mummified Head of Serial Killer 'The Vampire of Dusseldorf' [. . .] on Display in Wisconsin After Doctors Cut It Open to Find a Reason for His Evil." *Daily Mail*, July 9, 2018. www.dailymail.co.uk.

The Mitchell-Hedges Crystal Skull

Edwards, Owen. "The Smithsonian's Crystal Skull." Smithsonianmag.com, May 29, 2008. www.smithsonianmag.com.

Lovett, Richard A., and Scot Hoffman. "Crystal Skulls." *National Geographic*, January 2017. www.nationalgeographic.com.

The Miniature Coffins of Arthur's Seat

Dash, Mike. "Edinburgh's Mysterious Miniature Coffins." Smithsonianmag.com, April 15, 2013. www.smithsonianmag.com.

National Museums Scotland. "The Mystery of the Miniature Coffins: The XVII." Accessed November 2019. www.nms.ac.uk.

The Skin Book of James Allen

Allen, James. *Narrative of the Life of James Allen, Alias George Walton, Alias Jonas Pierce, Alias James H. York, Alias Burley Grove, the highwayman: Being His Death-Bed Confession, to the Warden of the Massachusetts State Prison*. Boston: Harrington, 1837.

Ehrengardt, Thibault. "Who Skinned James Allen? The 'Skin Book.'" Rare Book Hub. Accessed November 2019. www.rarebookhub.com.

The Antikythera Mechanism

The Antikythera Mechanism Research Project. "Frequently Asqued [*sic*] Questions."

Accessed November 2019. http://www.antikythera-mechanism.gr.

Marchant, Jo. "Decoding the Antikythera Mechanism, the First Computer." *Smithsonian*, February 2015. www.smithsonianmag.com.

VII. The Curse in the Machine

The Prague Orloj

Goukassian, Elena. "The History of One of the Oldest Astronomical Clocks in the World." *Hyperallergic*, February 2, 2018. www.hyperallergic.com.

Prague.eu. "History of the Astronomical Clock." Accessed November 2019. www.prague.eu.

The Hungarian Suicide Song

Mikkelson, David. "Gloomy Sunday Suicides." Snopes.com, updated May 23, 2007. www.snopes.com.

New York Times. "Rezsoe Seres Commits Suicide; Composer of 'Gloomy Sunday.'" January 14, 1968.

James Dean's Porsche 550 Spyder

The Auto Insider. "The Curse of James Dean's 'Little Bastard.'" *Jalopnik*, December 31, 2008. www.jalopnik.com.

Preovolos, Chris. "60 Years After James Dean's Death, 'Cursed' Car Mystery Continues." SFGate, updated September 30, 2015. www.sfgate.com.

0888-888-888

Daily Mail. "Mobile Phone Number 0888-888-888 Is Suspended After Every User Assigned to It Dies." Updated May 25, 2010. www.dailymail.co.uk.

Matyszczyk, Chris. "The Cell Phone Number Whose Owners All Die." *CNET*, May 27, 2010. www.cnet.com.

The Science of Cursed Objects

Rajagopal, Sundararajan. "The Nocebo Effect." Priory.com, September 2007. www.priory.com.

The *Berzerk* Video Game Cabinet

Kerch, Steve. "Heart in blamed in death of video game patron, 18." *Chicago Tribune*, April 27, 1982.

Wirtanen, Josh. "How Many People Has the Berzerk Arcade Game Killed?" *Retrovolve*, January 6, 2016. www.retrovolve.com.

Chain Emails

Collins, Paul. "You Must Forward This Story to Five Friends." *Slate*, October 1, 2010. www.slate.com.

Hayward, Alexandra. "Email This or Your Crush Will Die: The History of the Chain Letter." *Vice*, December 9, 2015. www.vice.com..

Index

M

N

O

P

Acknowledgments

I'm not sure if any of the below people want their names too closely associated with a book about cursed objects, but they helped me out a ton with it, so their bad.

I want to thank my wife, Lindsey, for accompanying me to see many of the objects in this book and for putting up with me bringing one into our home (and on our vacation). Jim Logan, who runs Sleepy Hollow Cemetery and who always shows me a good time there, but in this case for taking me to the Bronze Lady. Christian Haunton, for putting me on the trail of Little Mannie. John Zaffis, for that time he let me into the creepier parts of his house.

Rebecca Gyllenhaal, for starting the whole thing and sticking with me throughout, along with the crack team at Quirk for making this project more than a mere .docx: Ryan Hayes, Jane Morley (who worked wonders on the manuscript), John J. McGurk, Nicole De Jackmo, Jennifer Murphy, and Kate McGuire.

And, of course, Jon MacNair, whose illustrations by themselves are worth me writing this book and whose art you should look up right away.

I hereby absolve everyone on this page of any culpability and ensuing bad fortune you would have otherwise received from working on a project like this.

J. W. OCKER is a travel writer, novelist, and blogger. He is the author of the Edgar Award winning and Anthony Award nominated book *Poe-Land*. His other books include *A Season with the Witch*, *The New England Grimpendium*, and *The New York Grimpendium*. His writing can be found in the *Boston Globe*, the *Atlantic*, *Atlas Obscura*, and the *Guardian*, among other publications. He is also the creator of the blog and podcast *OTIS: Odd Things I've Seen*, where he chronicles his visits to oddities around the world. He has personally handled dozens of cursed objects yet miraculously lived to tell the tale.

R.I.P.

R.I.P.
R.I.P.
R.I.P.
R.I.P.
R.I.P.
R.I.P.